FLOATING DISTRICTS

GENOA

FLORIDA INTERNATIONAL UNIVERSITY ‖ MASTER PROJECT IN GENOA / LANDSCAPE ARCHITECTURE IN GENOA

SPRING 2019

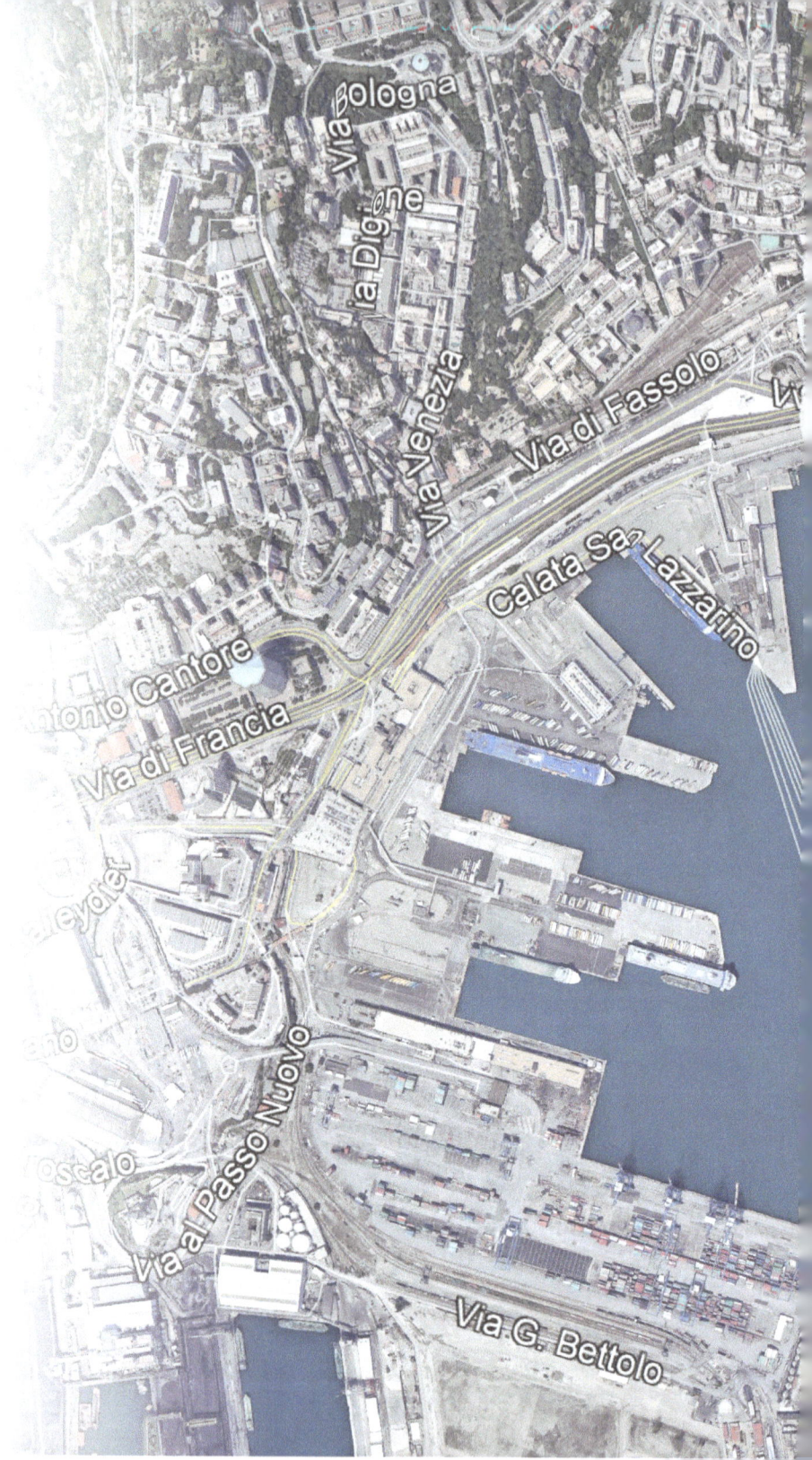

Florida International University Faculty

Eric Peterson   Senior Instructor

Ebru Ozer   Visiting Instructor LAEUD

Thomas Spiegelhalter   Visiting Instructor ARC

Elisa Cagelli   Architecture Studio Critic

Adriana Ghersi   Landscape Architecture Studio Critic

Designers

Josmanny Cid   Landscape Architecture in Genoa

Ramses Terrero   Master Project in Genoa

Collaboration of all Drawings

GENOA
SPRING
2019

004

TABLE OF CONTENT

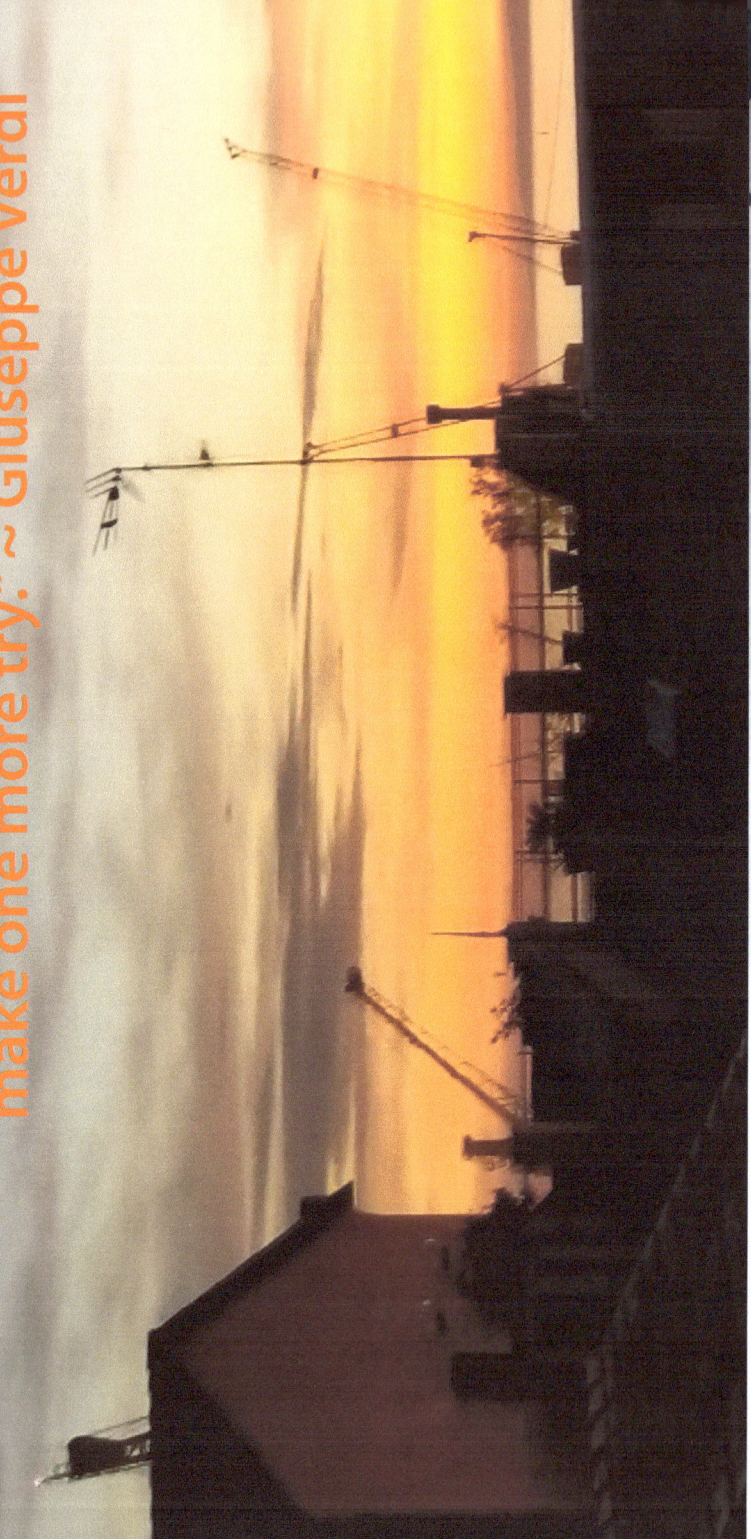

GENOA

//// To copy the truth can be a good thing, but to invent the truth is better, much better." ~ Giuseppe Verdi

//// I have striven for perfection, it has alwa eluded me, but I surely had an obligation make one more try." ~ Giuseppe Verdi

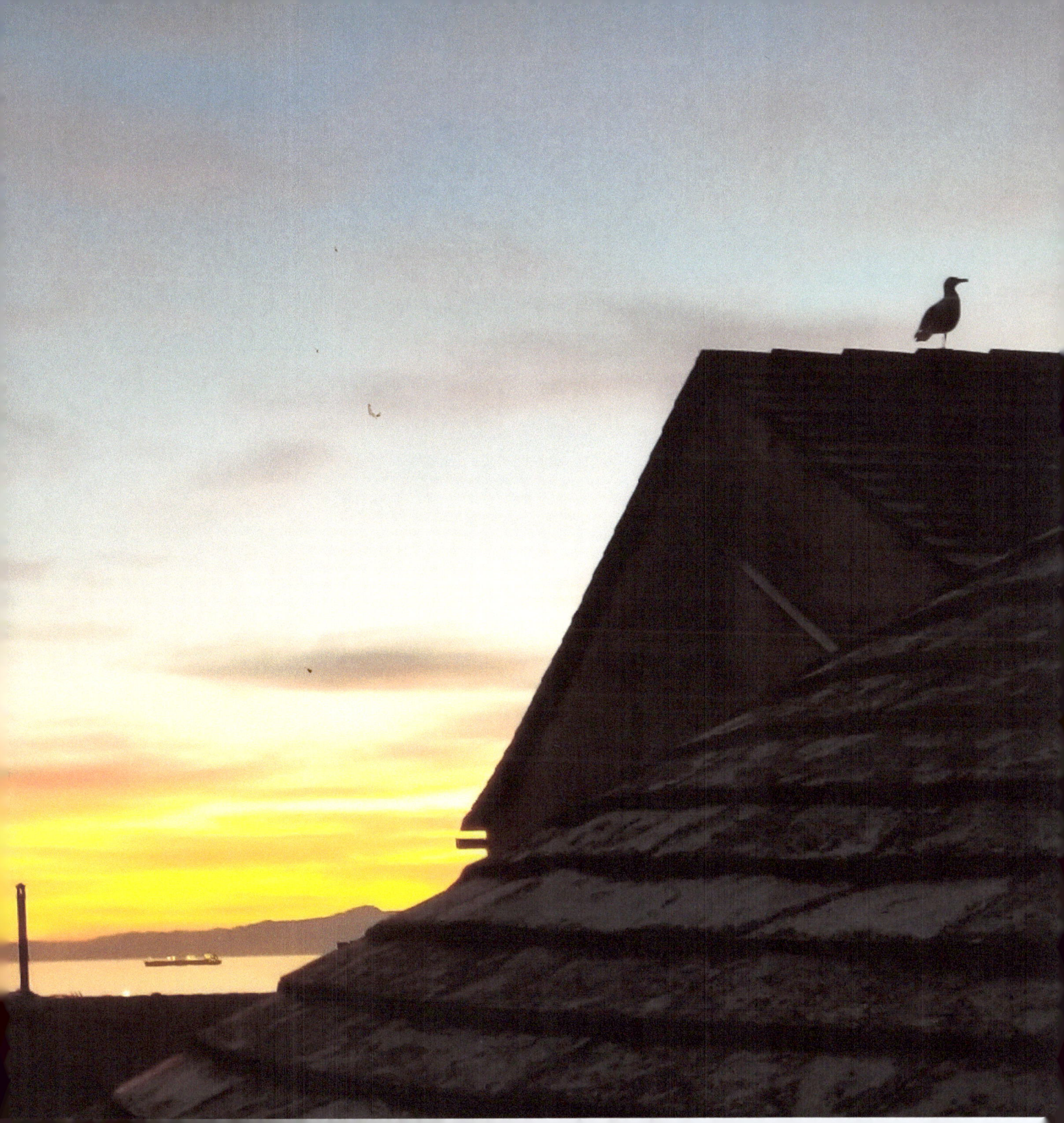

Historic edge of Molo

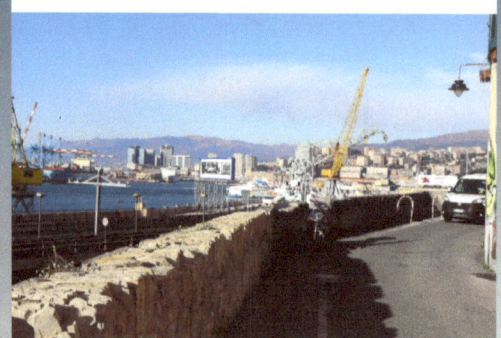

Porto Antico

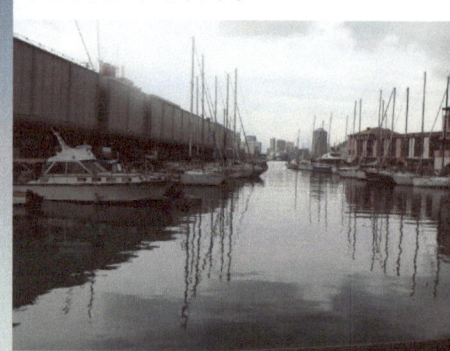

San Lorenzo Exterior

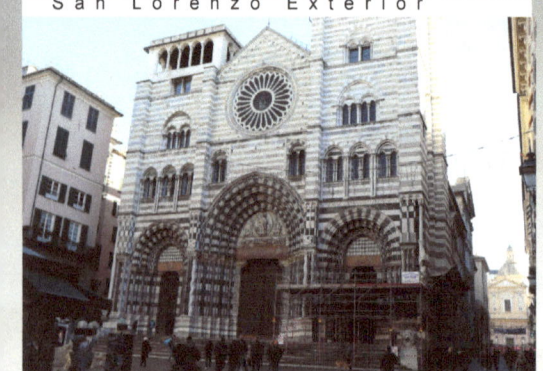

San Lorenzo Detail

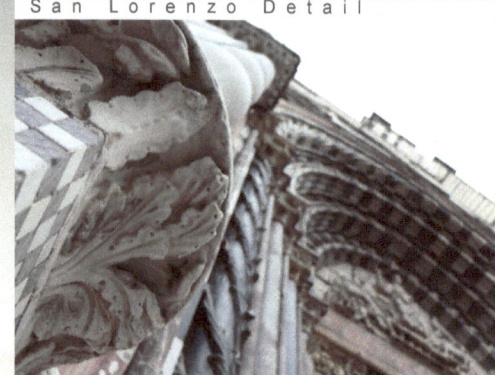

San Lorenzo Detail

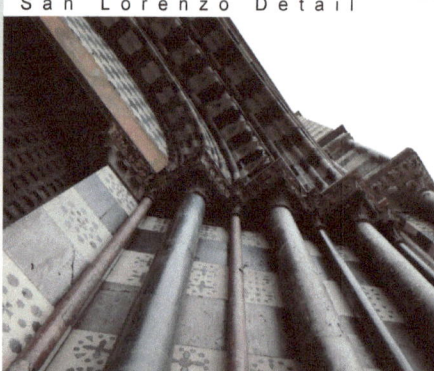

Interior of San Lorenzo

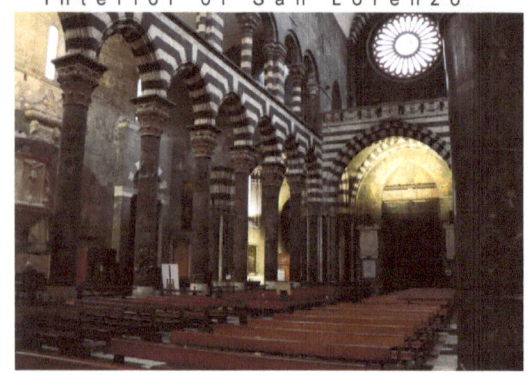

Interior of San Lorenzo

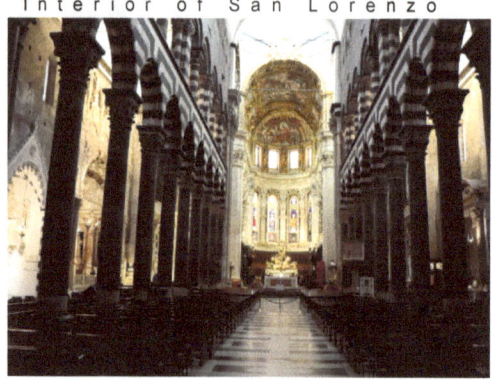

Piazza de Ferrari

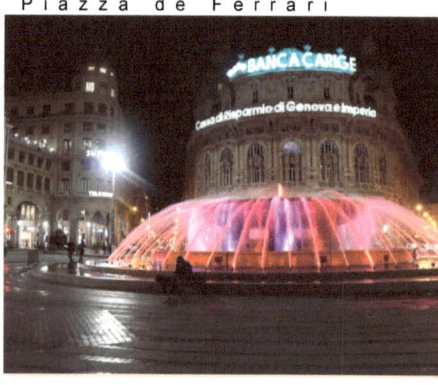

Arcades- via XX Settembre

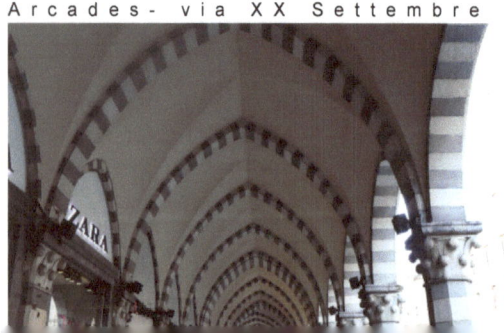

Arcades- via XX Settembre

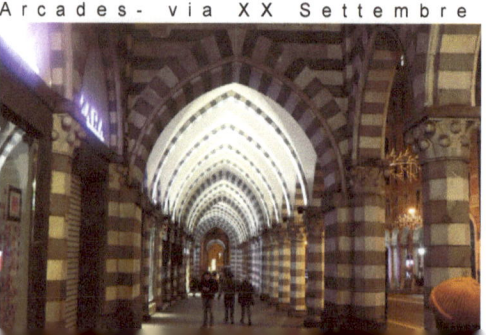

Gate tower threshold

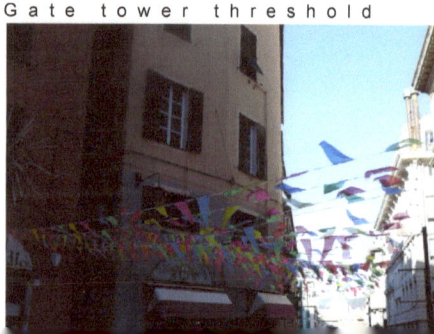

Modern Genoa

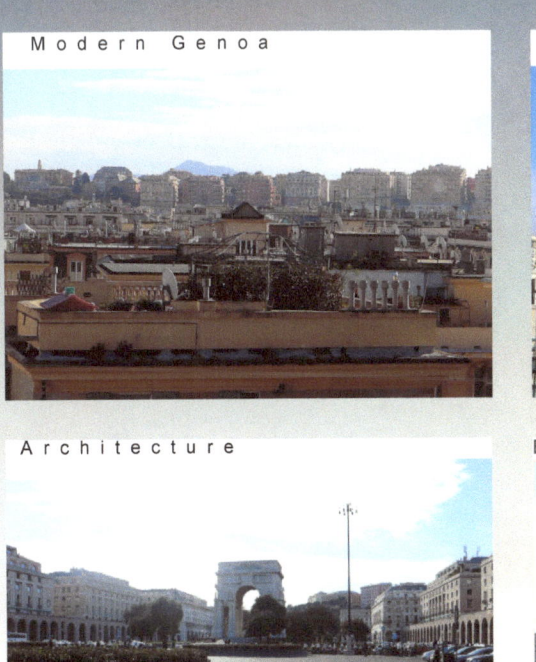

Bridge above Settembre

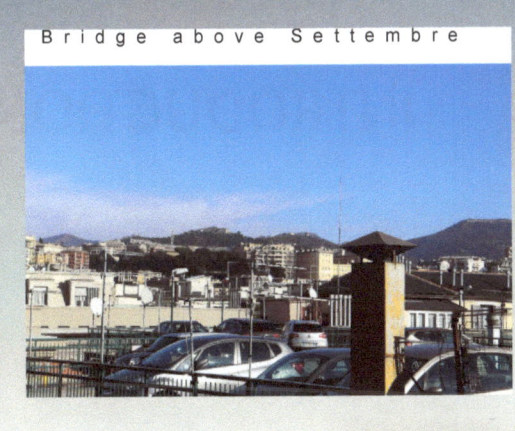

View from Saint Maria Consulate "S

Images by: Josmanny Cid

GENOA

Architecture

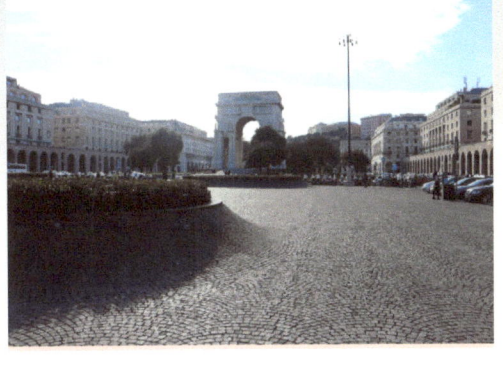

Bridge Park

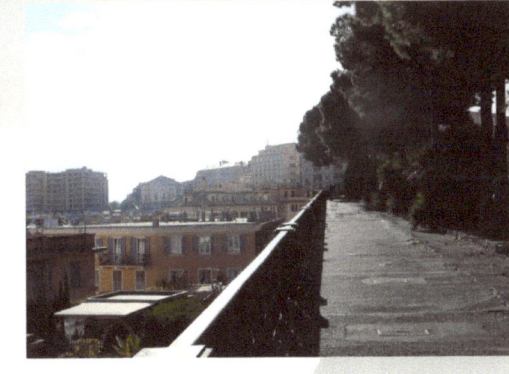

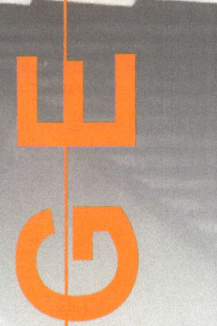

Via XX Settembre

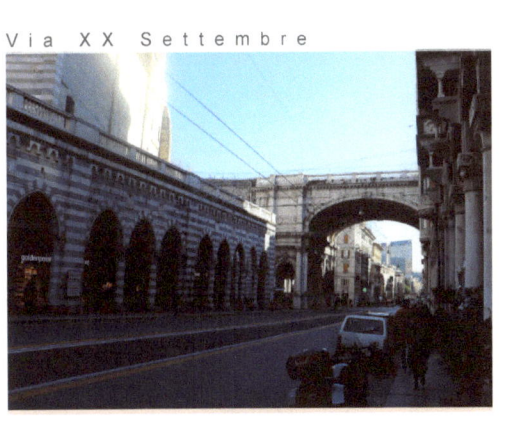

Via XX Settembre

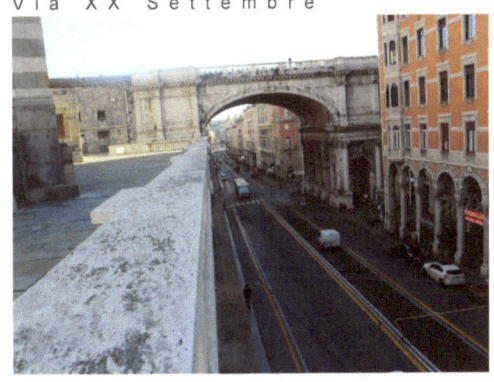

Wall Detail

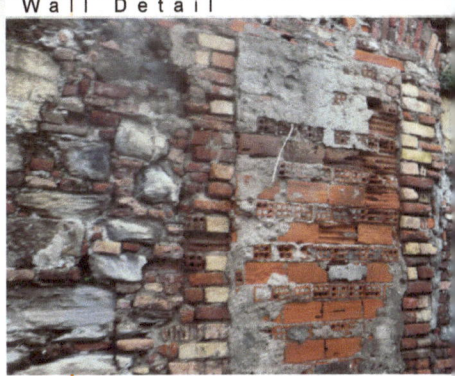

Gate tower threshold

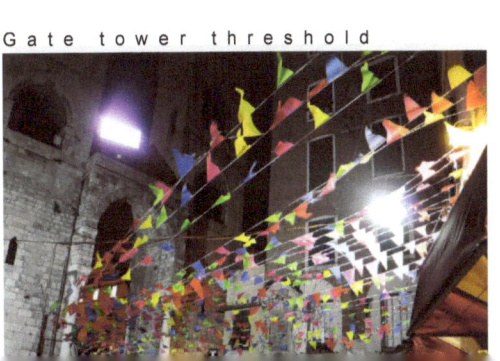

Arcades- via XX Settembre

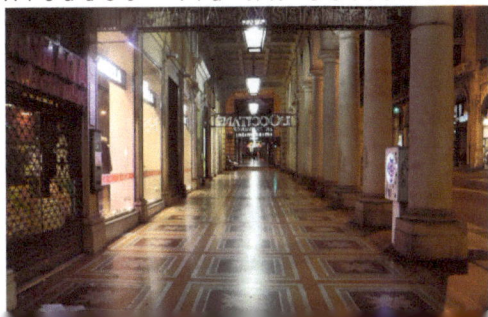

Wall detail

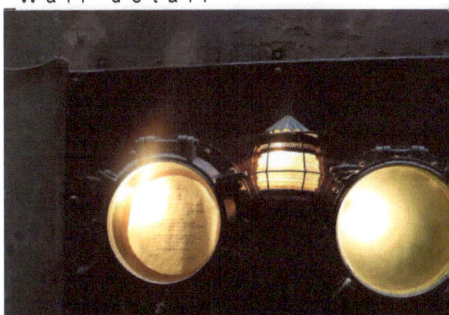

INTRODUCTION

With the city of Genoa and its Mediterranean seaport having a substantial impact to the peoples way of life in a port city. Genoa also has a history of a diverse languages of Medieval, Renaissance, Baroque, and Gothic Architecture all throughout the city. The project began as a redevelopment of the historic part of Genoa called the Molo. The Molo has a variety of mix used elements like Industrial,commercial, and Governmental buildings that have become the sites main attraction through the years. With the Molo , but the most important element that the Molo is missing is a waterfront edge or experience for the Genovesse people. With the edge of the water used to being at the fort walls of the molo, Genoa's very own Architect Renzo Piano has took action with creating a blue line plan that creates a channel that extends all the way from the Porto Antico to the fair. With Renzo Piano's Blueprint being a main design component to the edge with Genoa's dense fabric of districts, topography, and culture.

In addition, exploring the city of Genoa and traveling to other major cities in Italy gave me a synopsis on how people, culture, and the environment tie into a city. Traveling to major cities, like Florence , Venice , Verona, Rome, Switzerland, Stuttgart, Basel,

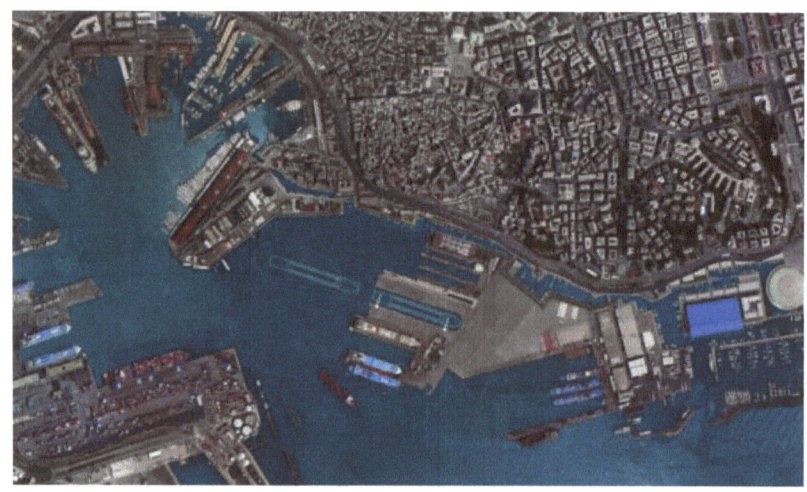

Renzo Piano's Blueprint for Genoa
http://tiny.cc/o66o5ye.

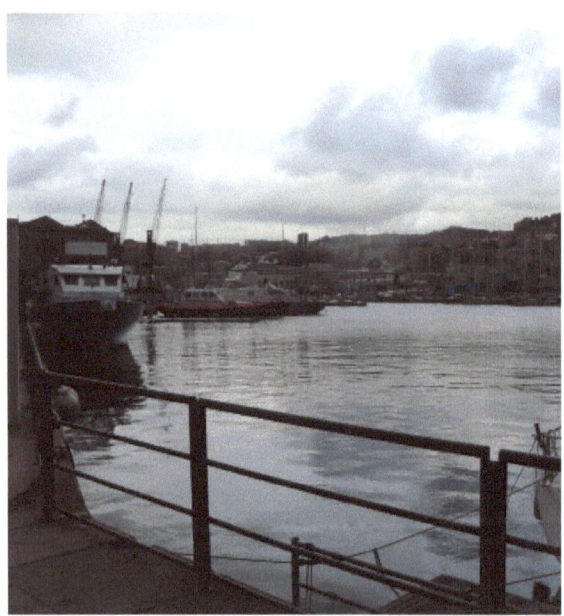
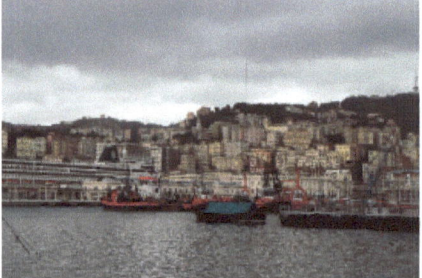
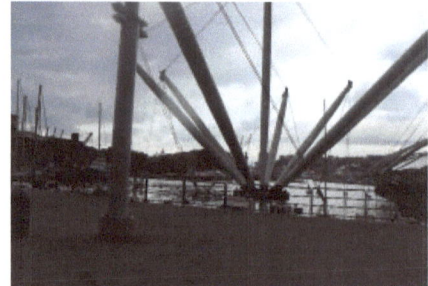
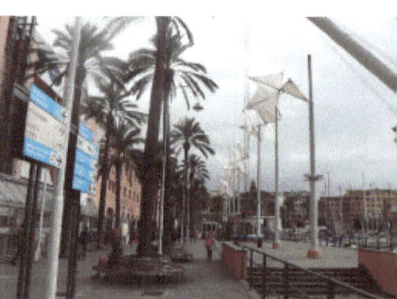
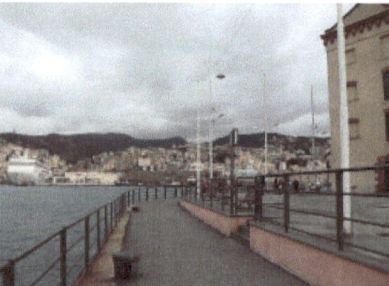

HISTORY

Genoa was a precursor to the city states of Hong Kong and Singapore. They developed a leading shipping industry that extended across the Mediterranean world.

As for Genoa's Economy being the major element that brought prosperity to the city, it's politics has become its undoing throughout history. Factionalism and oligarchy has brought Genoa in decline. As for the ruling consuls at the time when Genoa's status of government was destroying the city, they were concerned with destroying each other rather than expanding the city for the future.

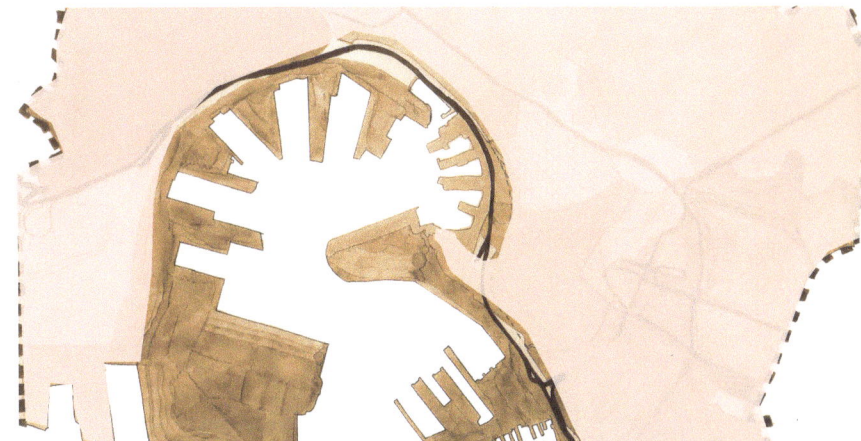

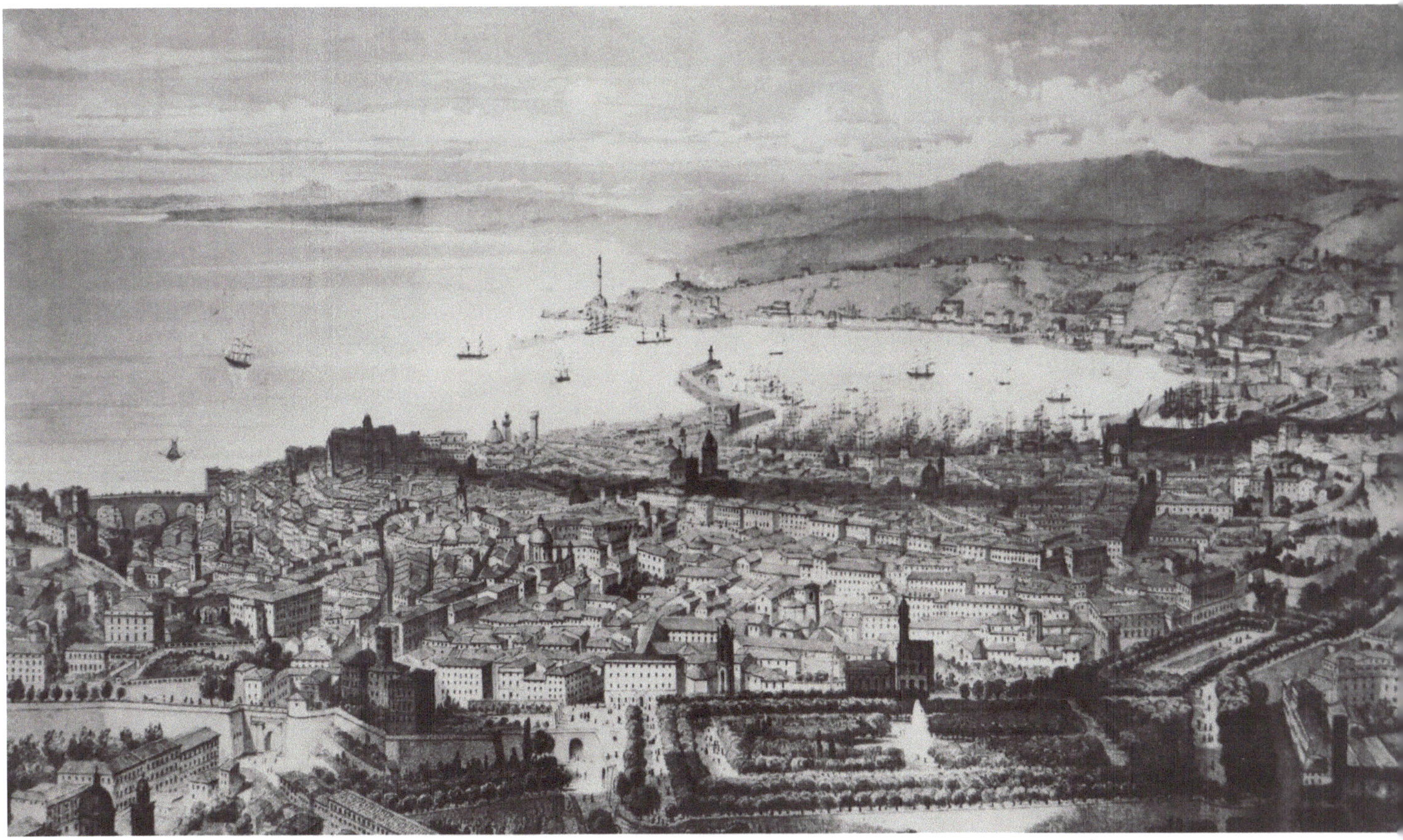

Genoa's old port image 1800's
Banco de Saint Gorge

CONTEXT

Genoa is a port city and it;s known for its central role in maritime trade over many centuries. Narrow lanes open onto monumental squares like Piazza de Ferrari, site of an iconic bronze fountain and Teatro Carlo Felice opera house. Certain piazza's have a variety of mix use spaces that create an experience for the people of Genoa.

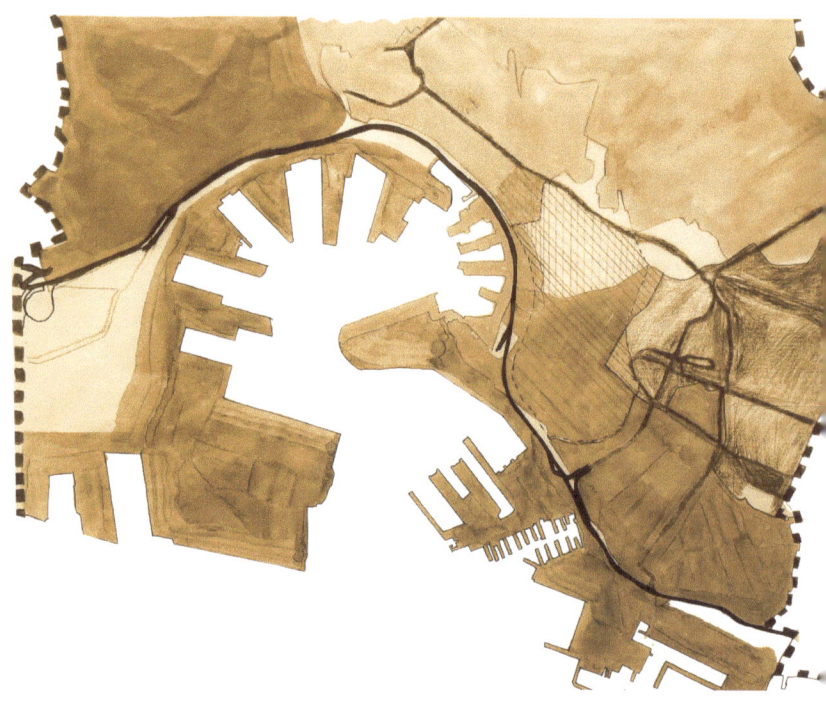

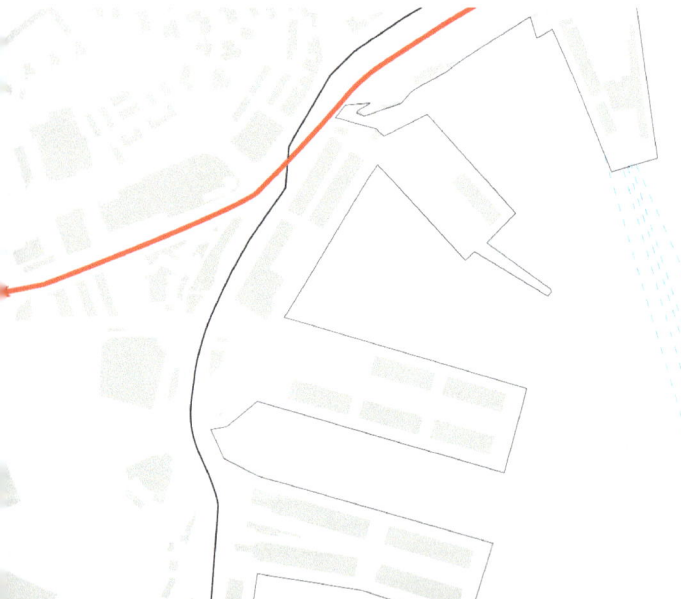

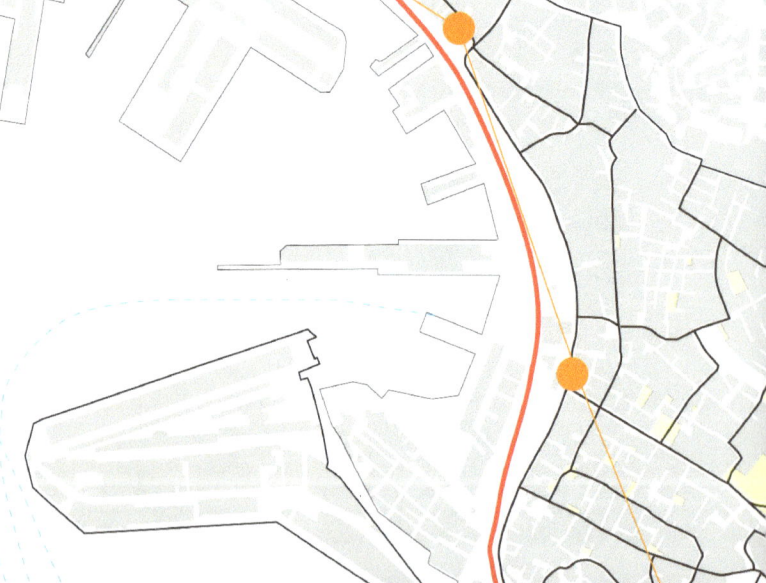

SITE

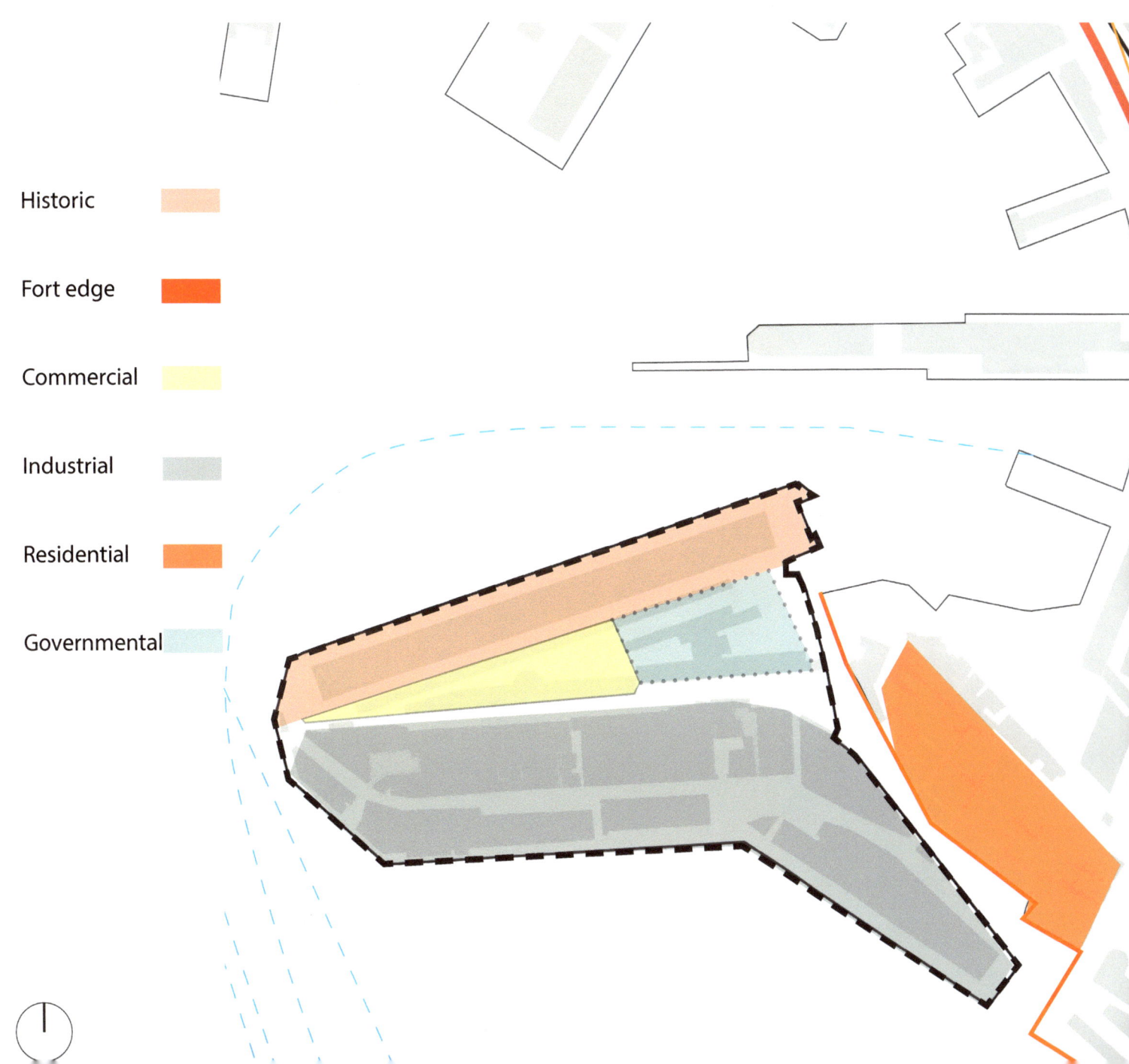

Historic

Fort edge

Commercial

Industrial

Residential

Governmental

SITE ANALYSIS
Context

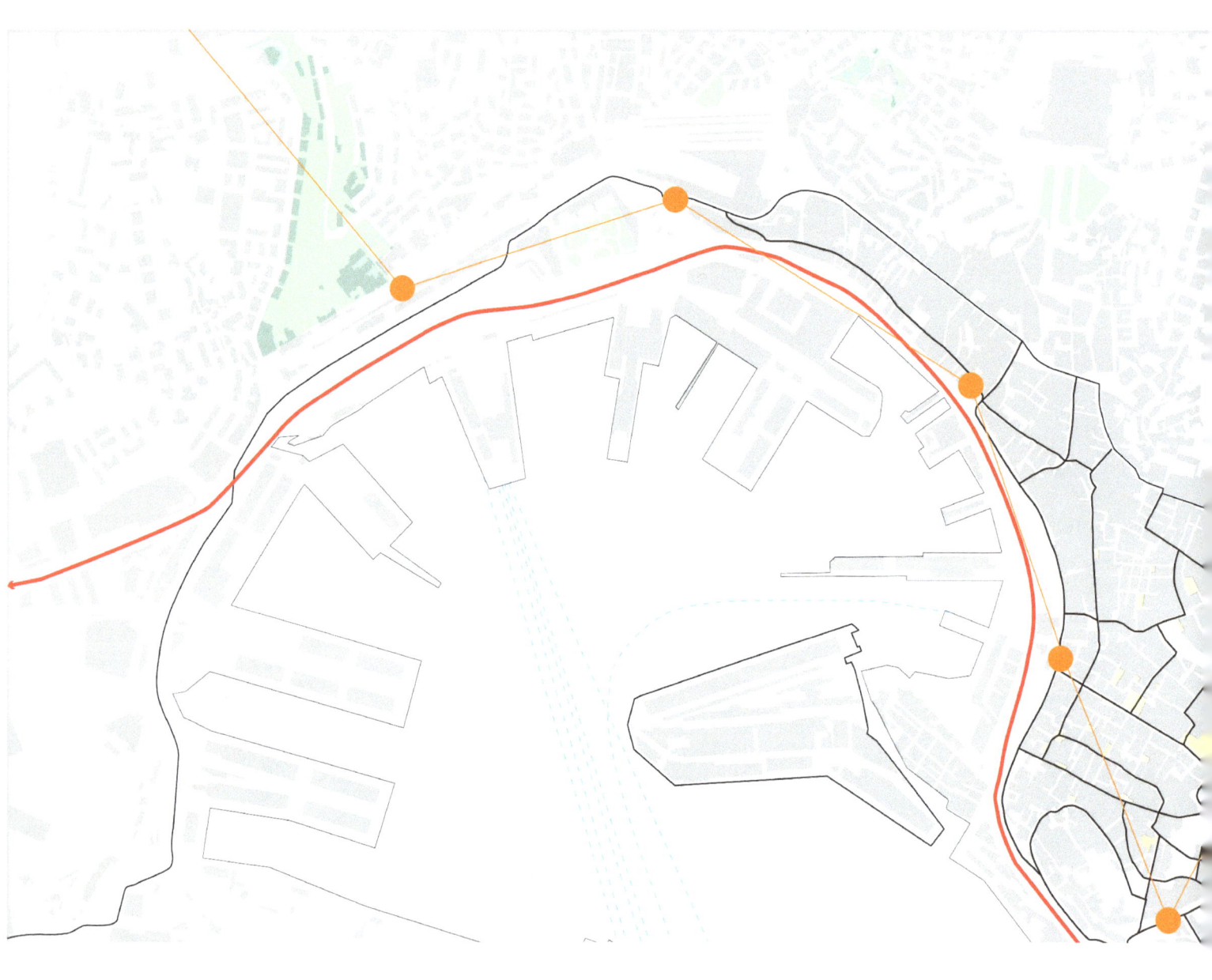

Metro   Piazza   Highway   Port Circulation   Parks

DISTRICTS

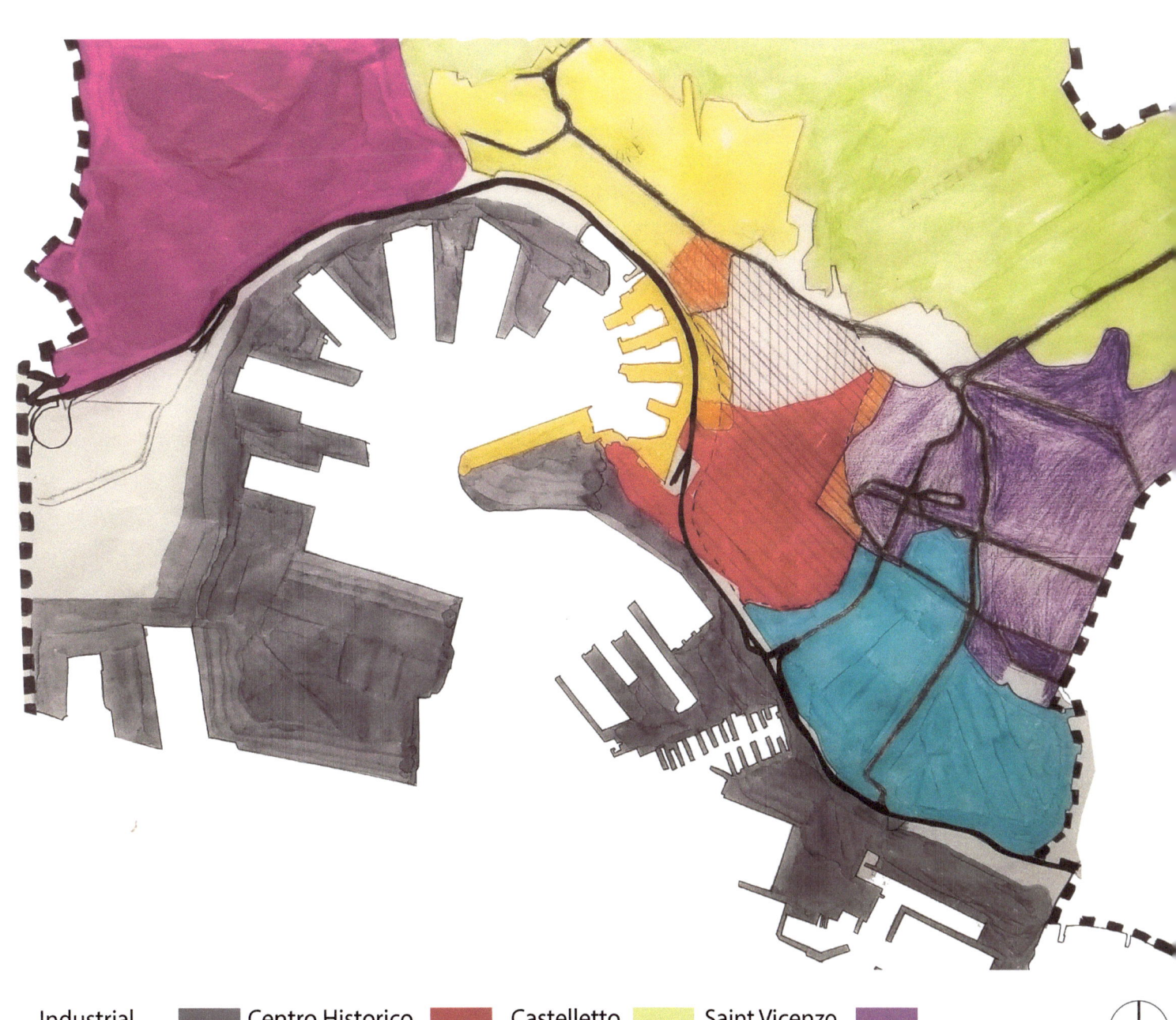

Industrial　　[   ]　　Centro Historico　　[   ]　　Castelletto　　[   ]　　Saint Vicenzo　　[   ]

Porto Antico　　[   ]　　Pre'　　[   ]　　Carignano　　[   ]　　San Teodoro　　[   ]

THE FLOATING DISTRICT
An addition to Renzo Piano's Blueprint

The Project is a redevelopment in the ancient port of Genoa. The main goal is to create public space and a mix use Cruise ship Terminal in a industrial zoned area that will become a brownfield.

The main concept of the project as a whole is to create an experience for the people of genova with the existing historic site's bands stretching out towards the waters edge. The bands in a way are a release from the series of boundaries, and dense fabric of Genoa, which creates an urban park with distinct areas, paths, and native vegetation to create a floating effect for a roof like structure with programmatic spaces underneath. In addition,Creating a microclimate for a ground condition, terminal, maritime museum, mix used residential building and a site connected urban park with programs throughout.

Due to the raised condition of sea level rise we were able to create public spaces underneath and in between each of the buildings, public events, and a variety of ground conditions that are for activity, and leisure.

The Terminal is a simple C shape which creates framed views of the water and the large atrium spaces piercing through the building as people flow in and out. Large Industrial cranes suspend the roof recalling the industrial heritage of the site and paying homage to the industrial waterfront.

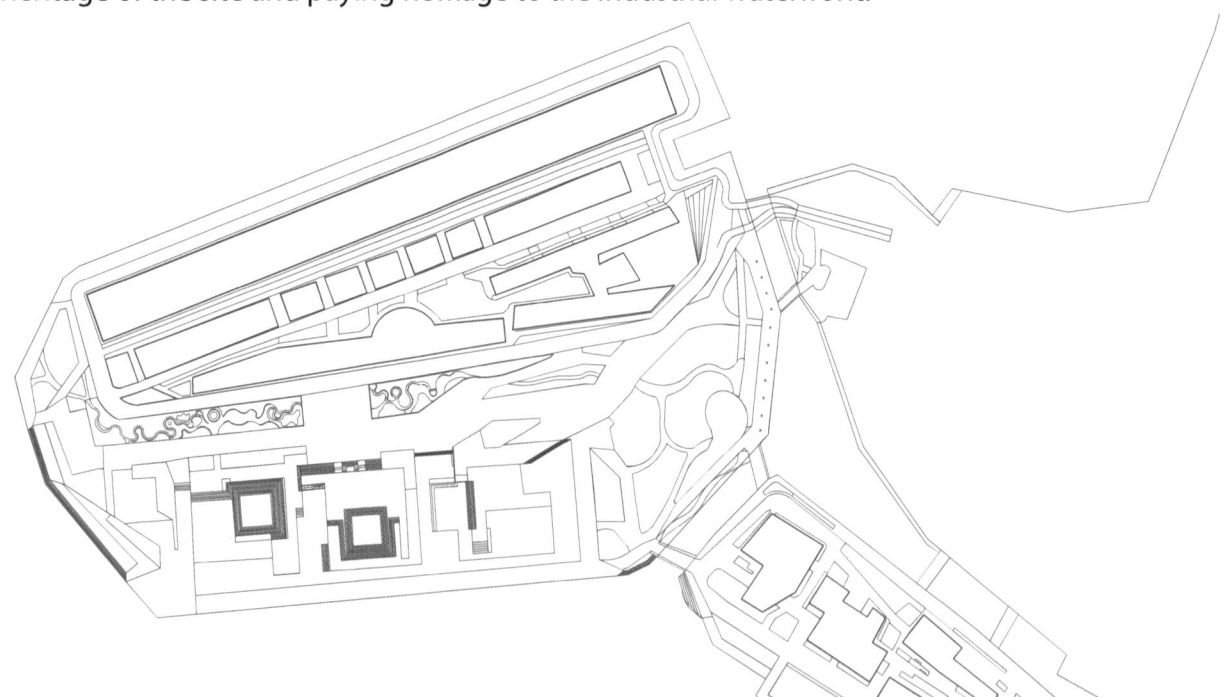

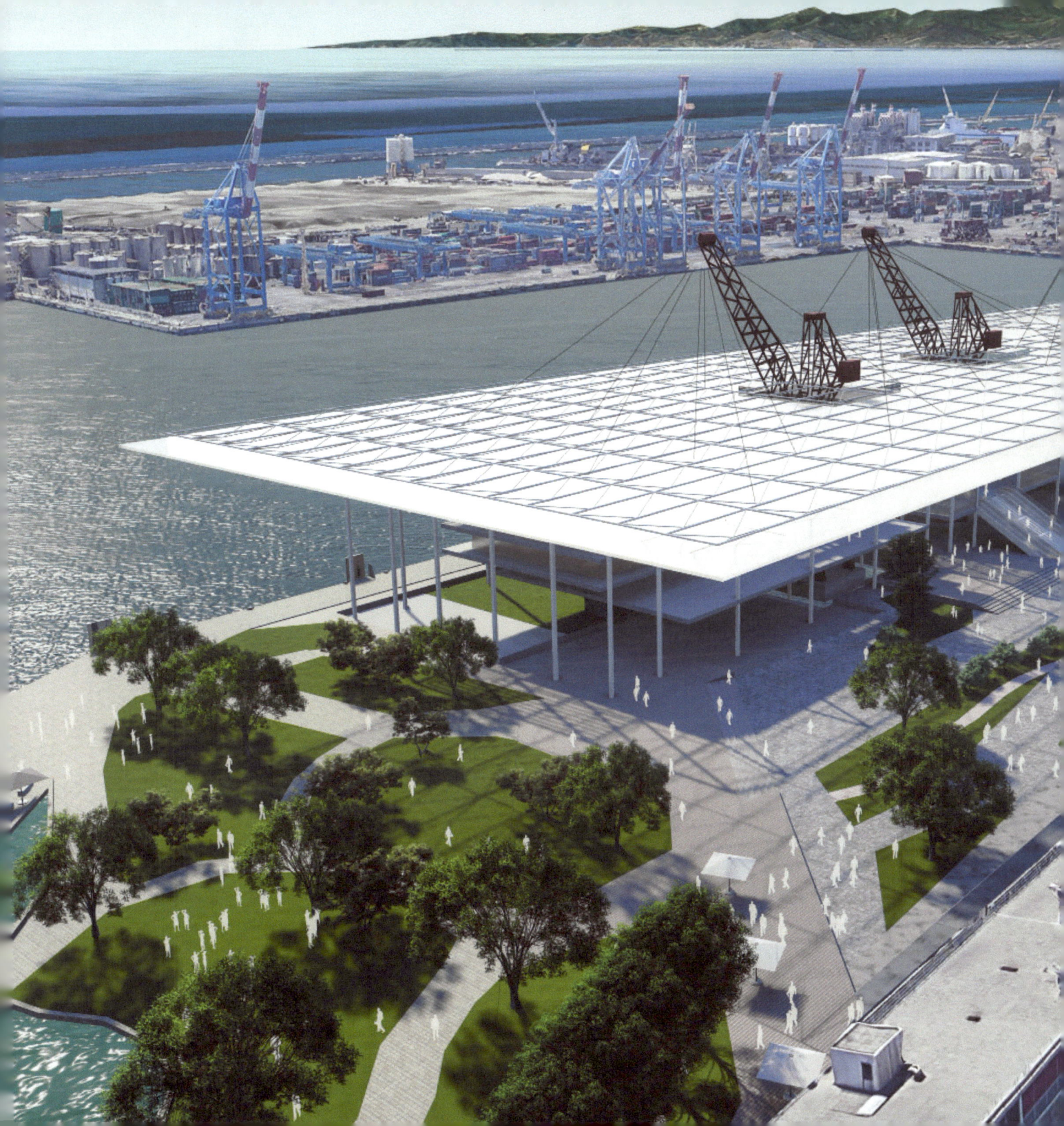

SITE PLAN

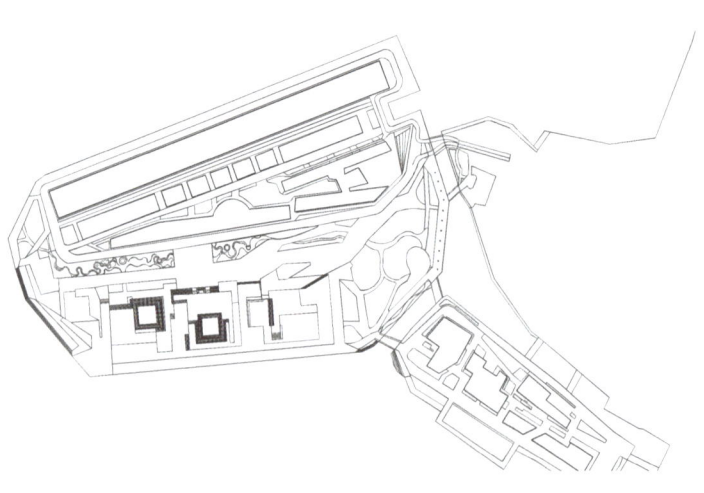

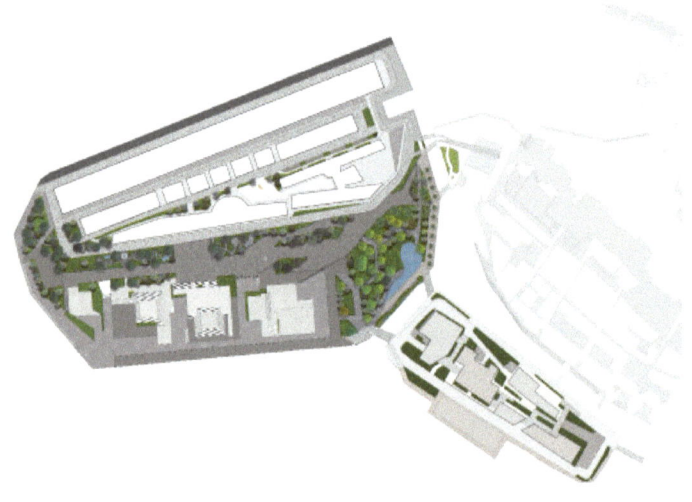

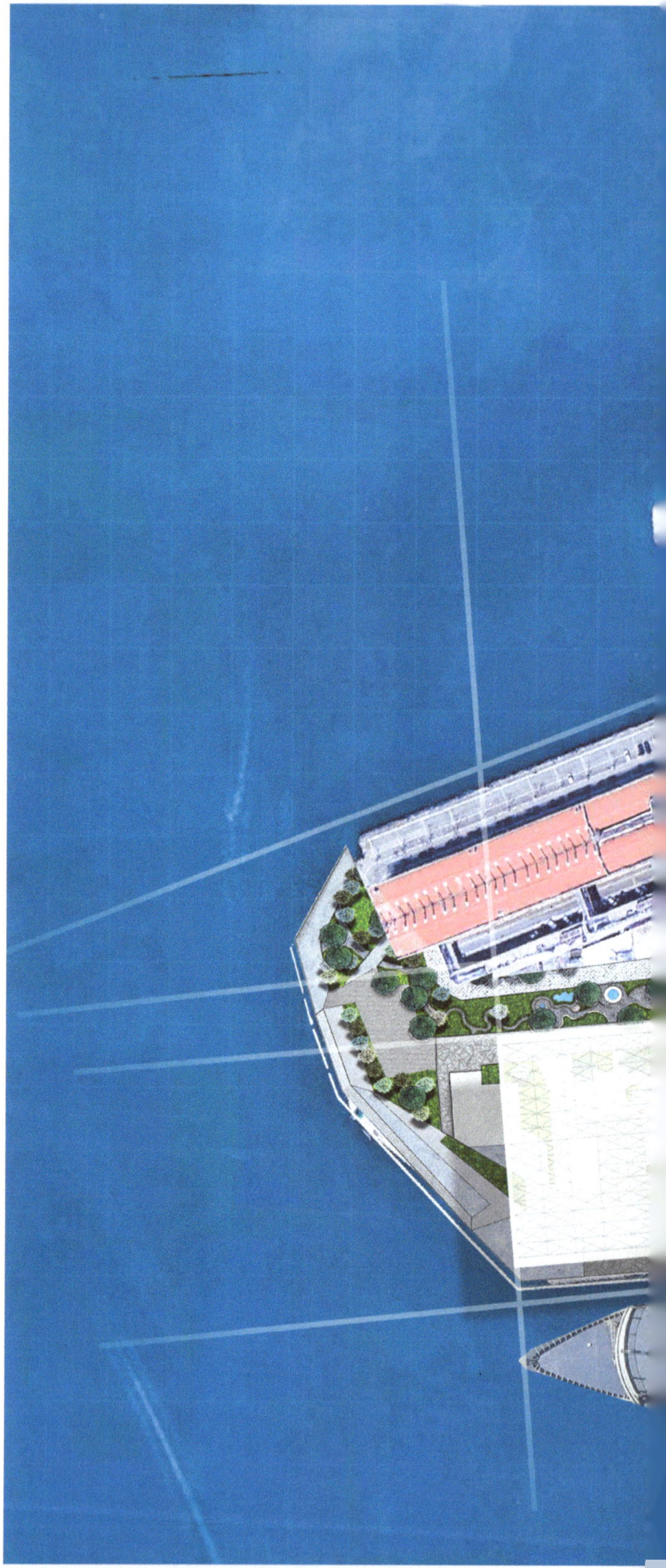

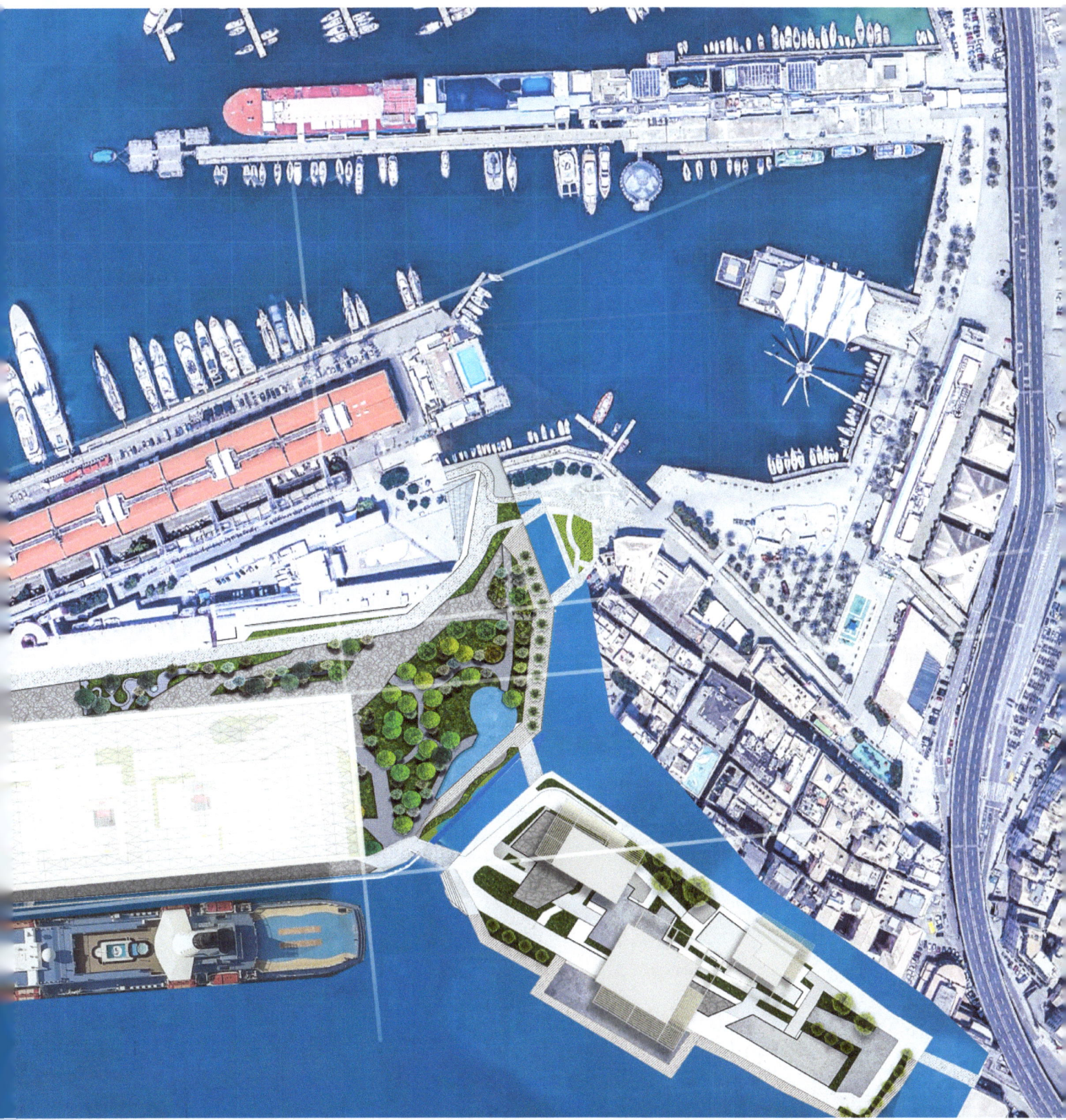

DIAGRAMS

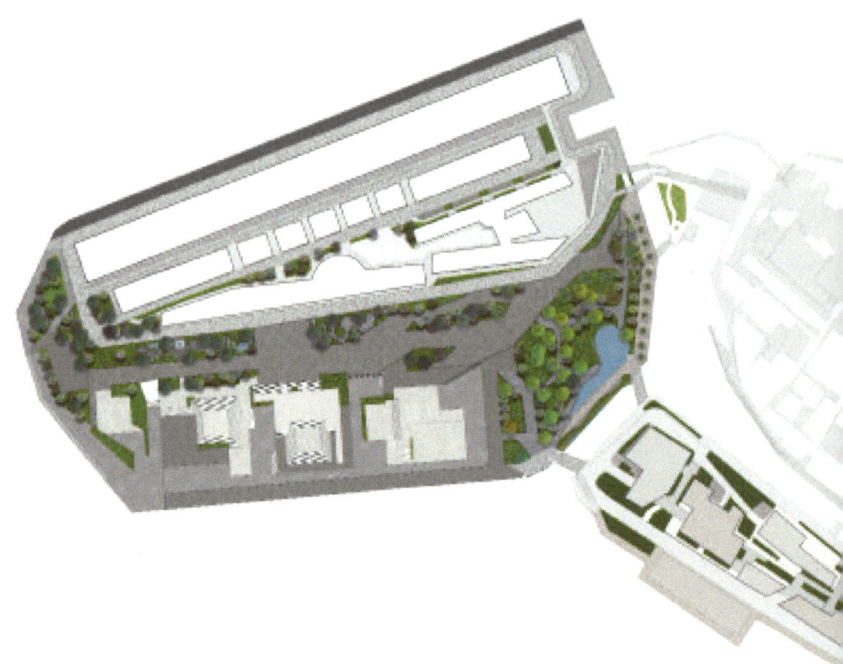

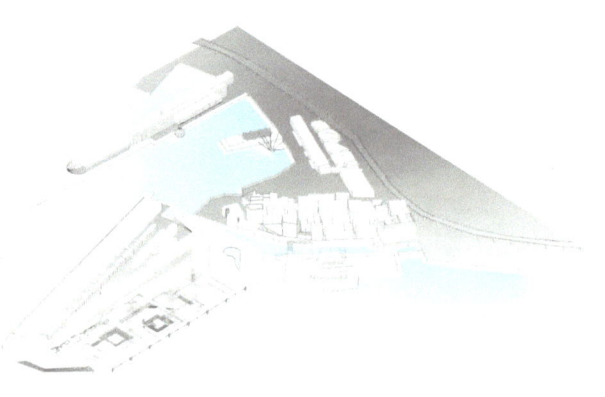

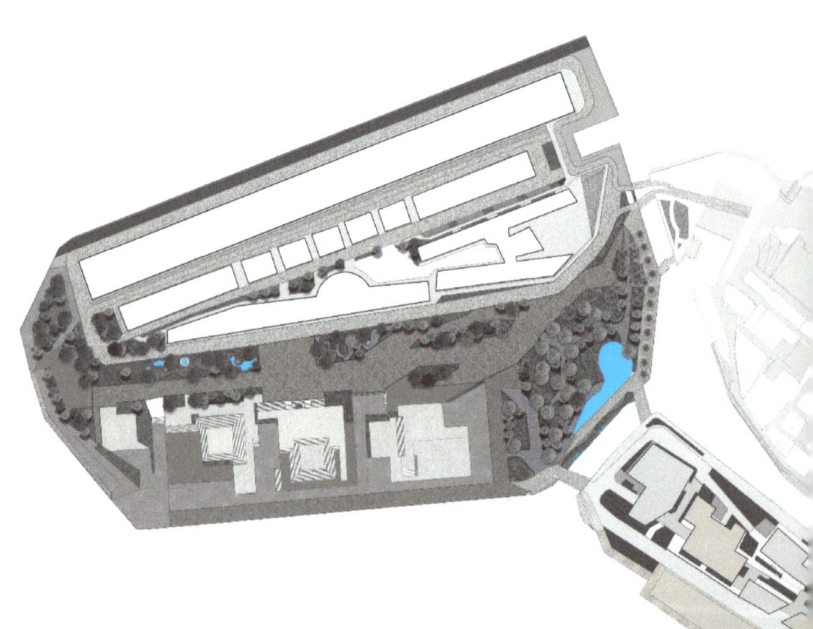

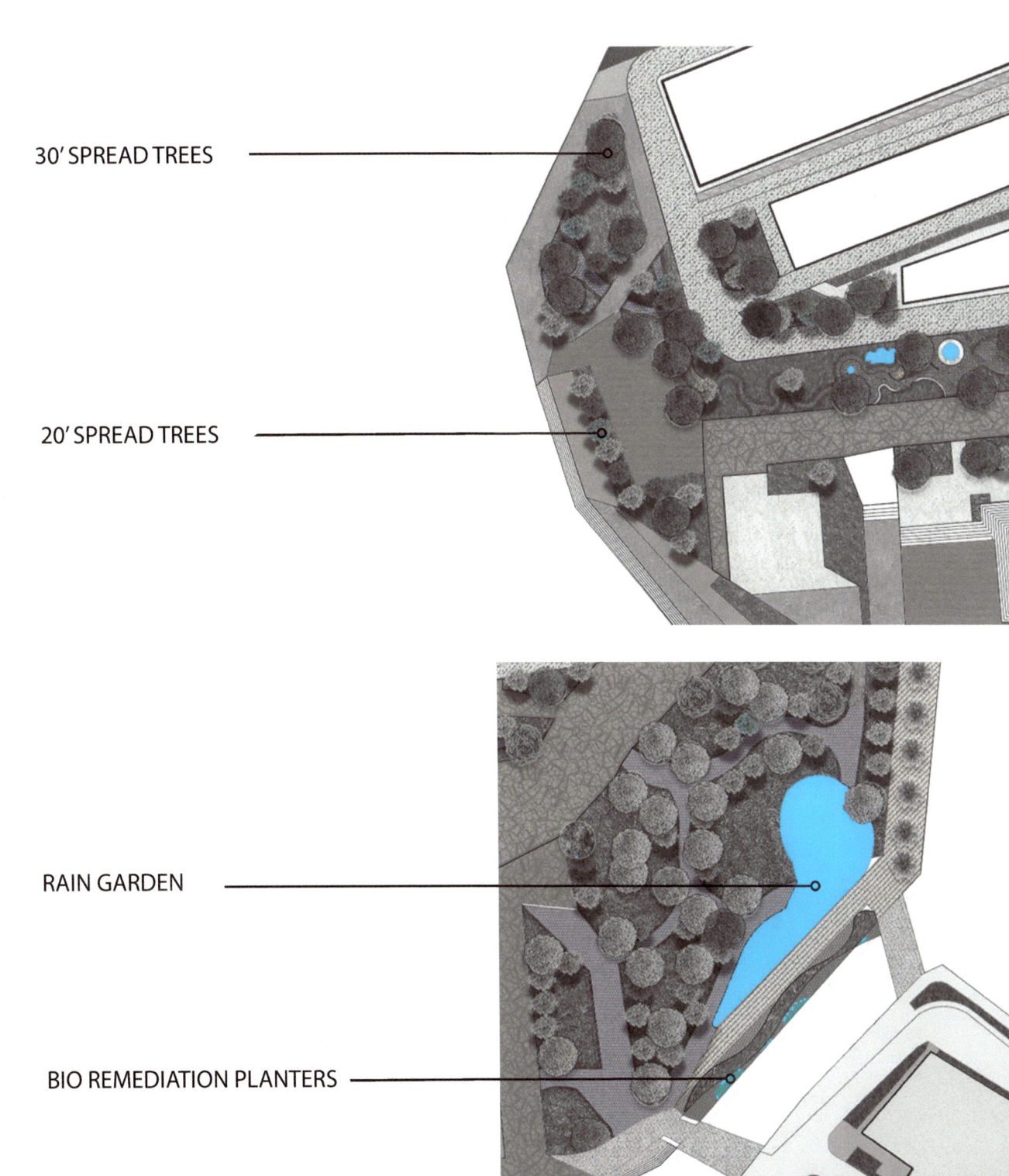

30' SPREAD TREES

20' SPREAD TREES

RAIN GARDEN

BIO REMEDIATION PLANTERS

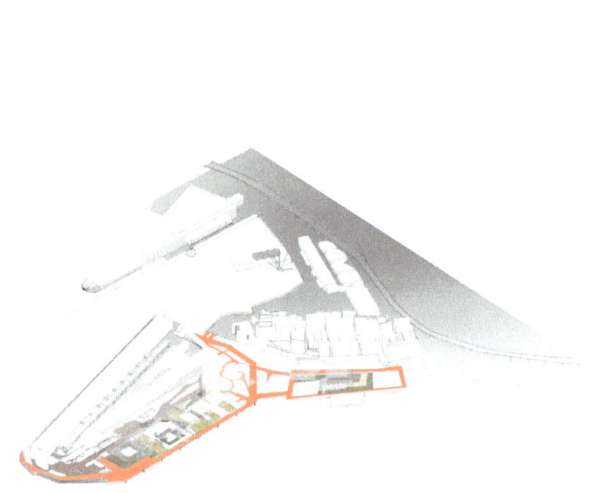

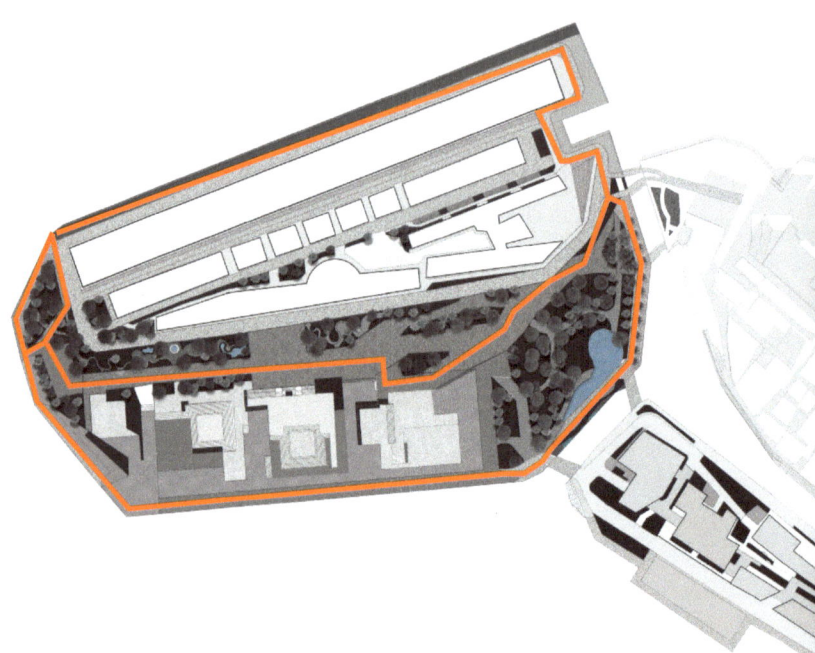

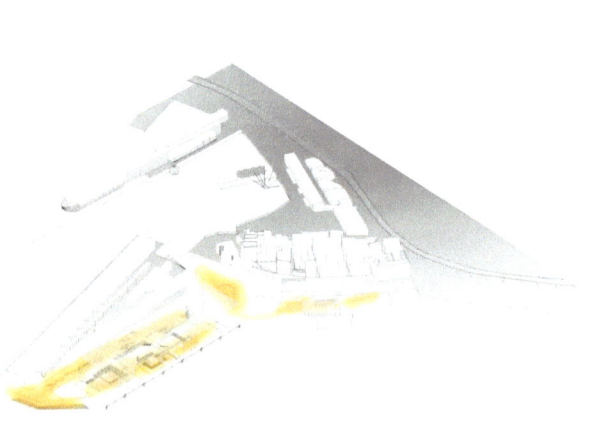

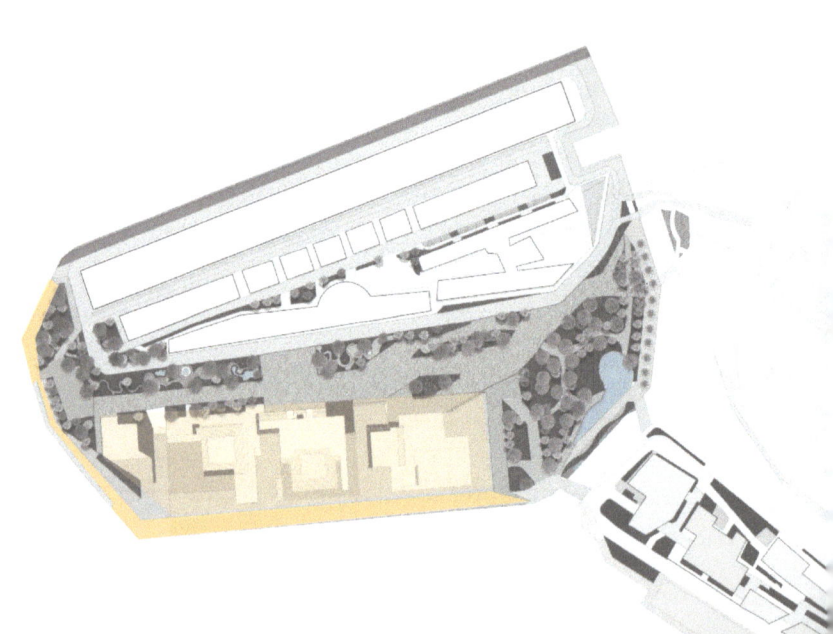

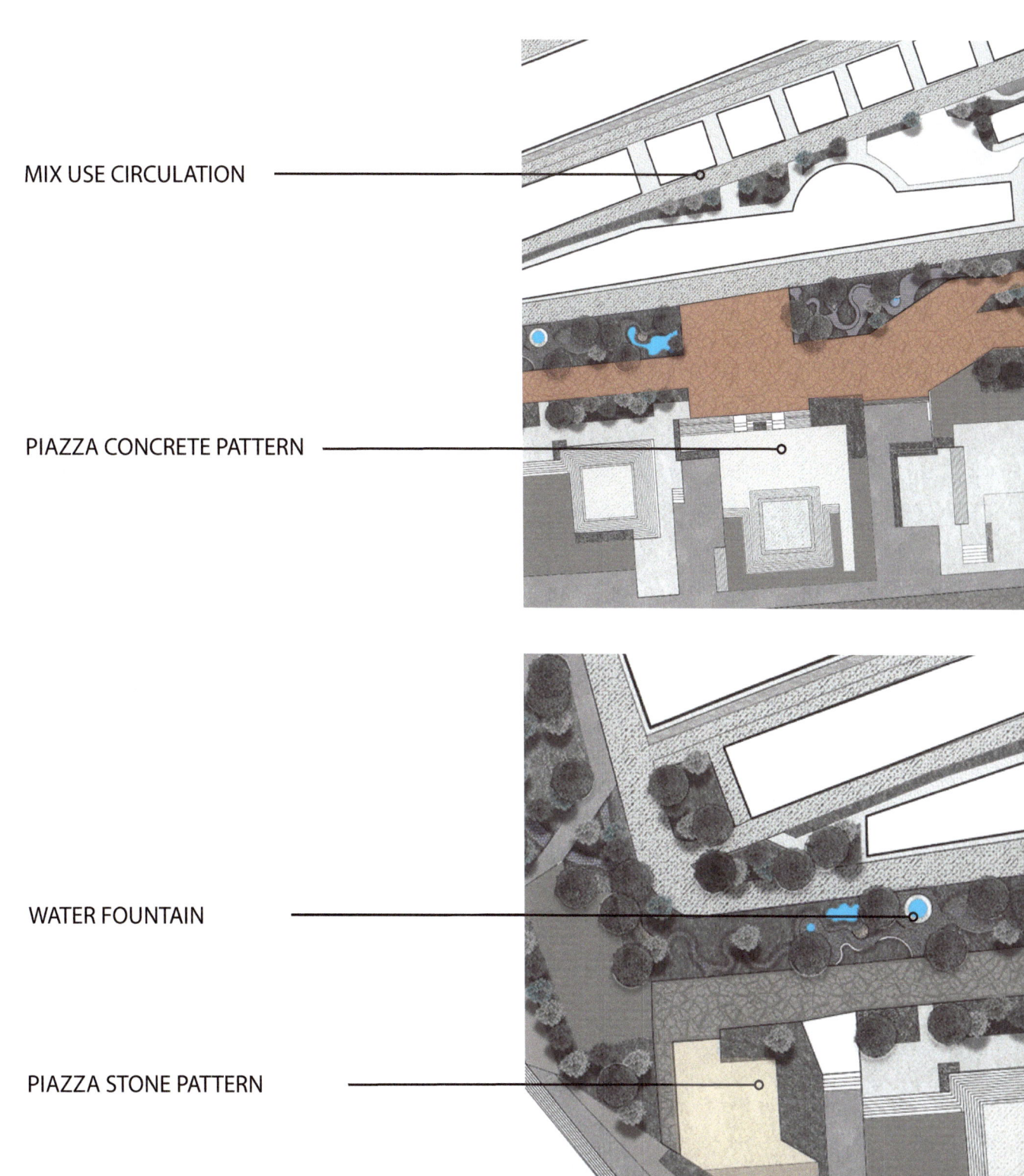

MIX USE CIRCULATION

PIAZZA CONCRETE PATTERN

WATER FOUNTAIN

PIAZZA STONE PATTERN

PUBLIC SPACE

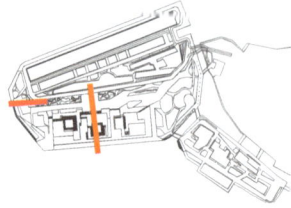

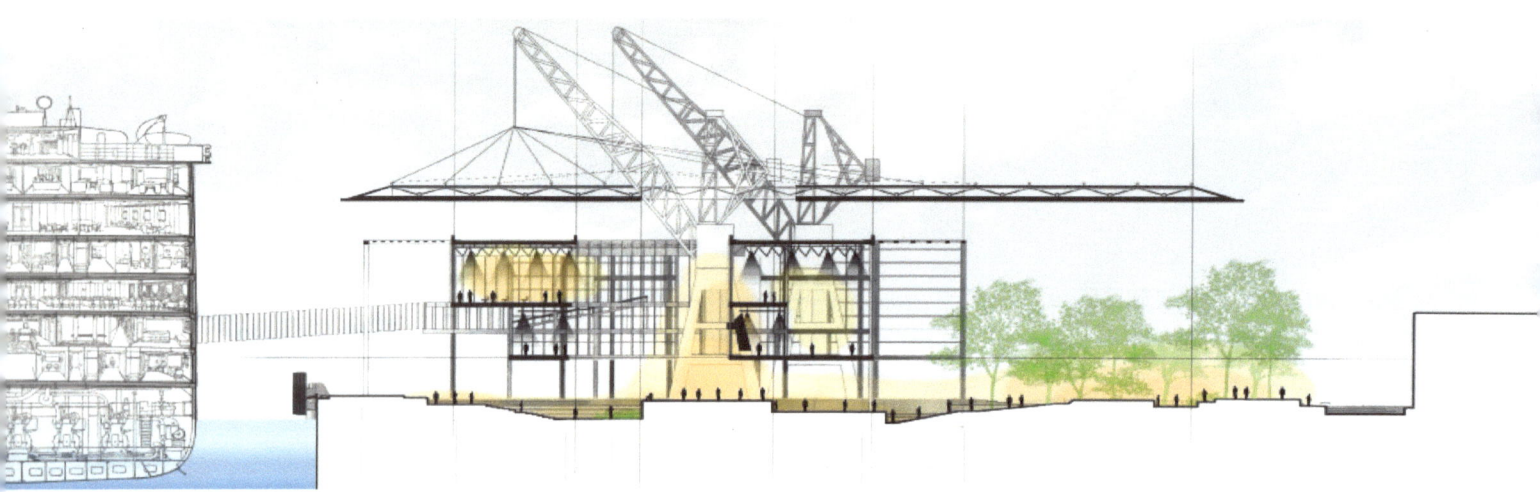

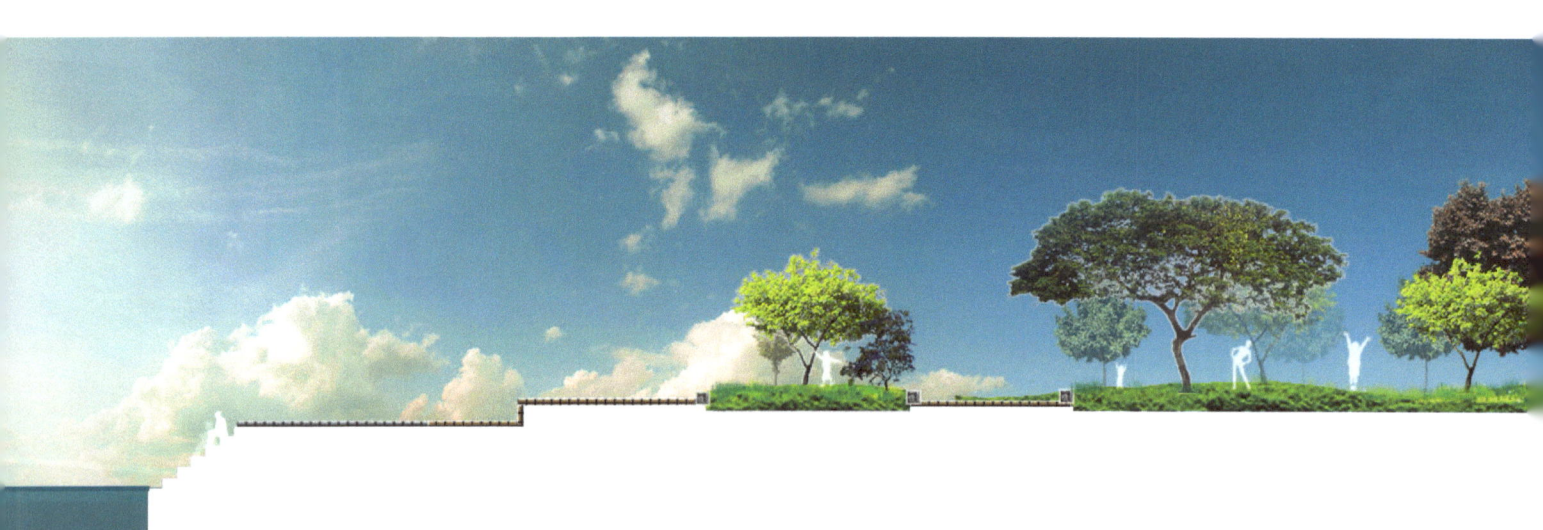

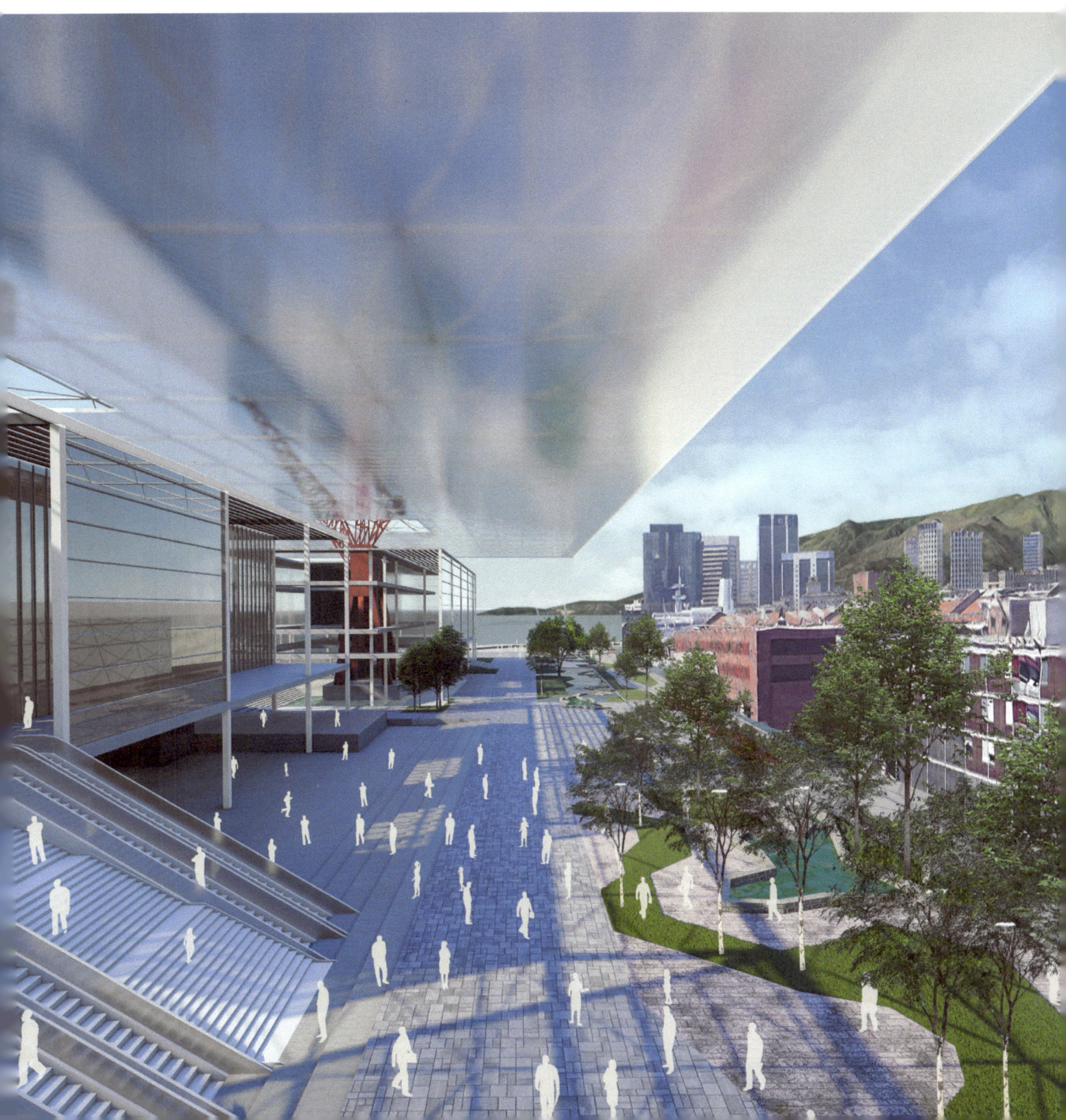

PUBLIC ATRIUM

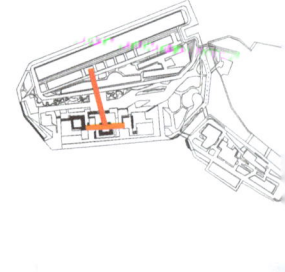

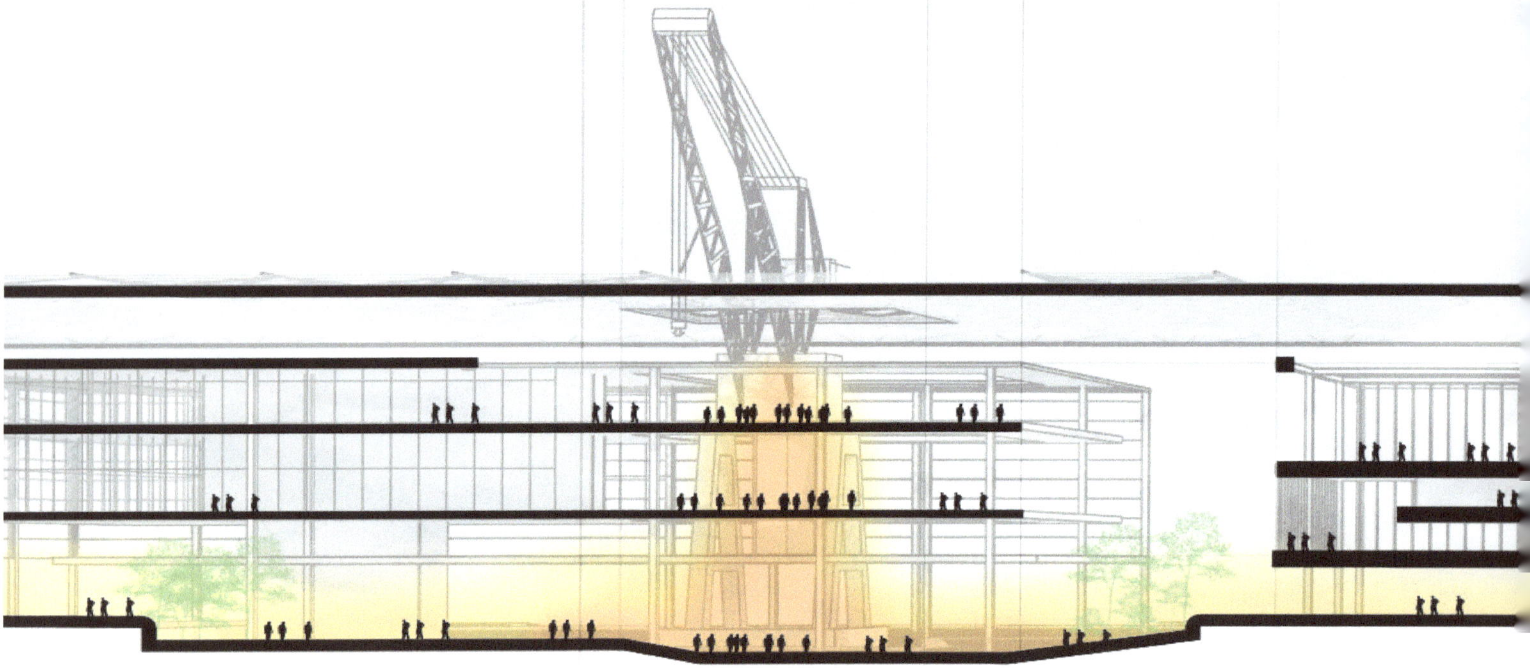

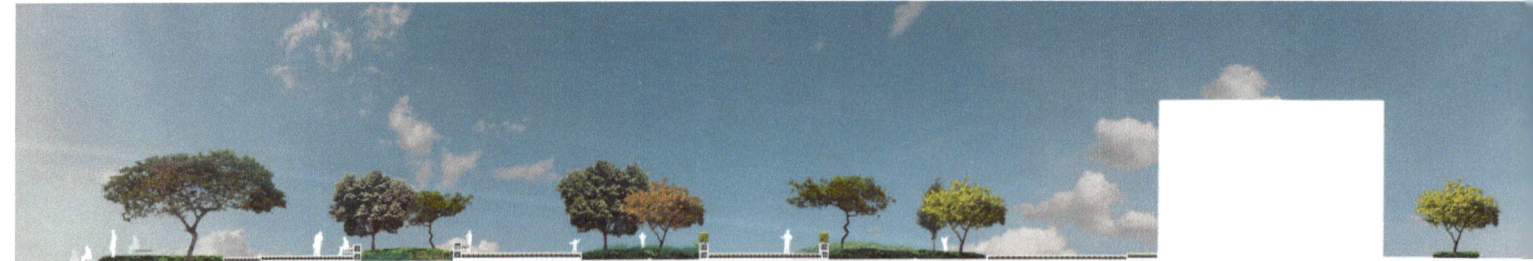

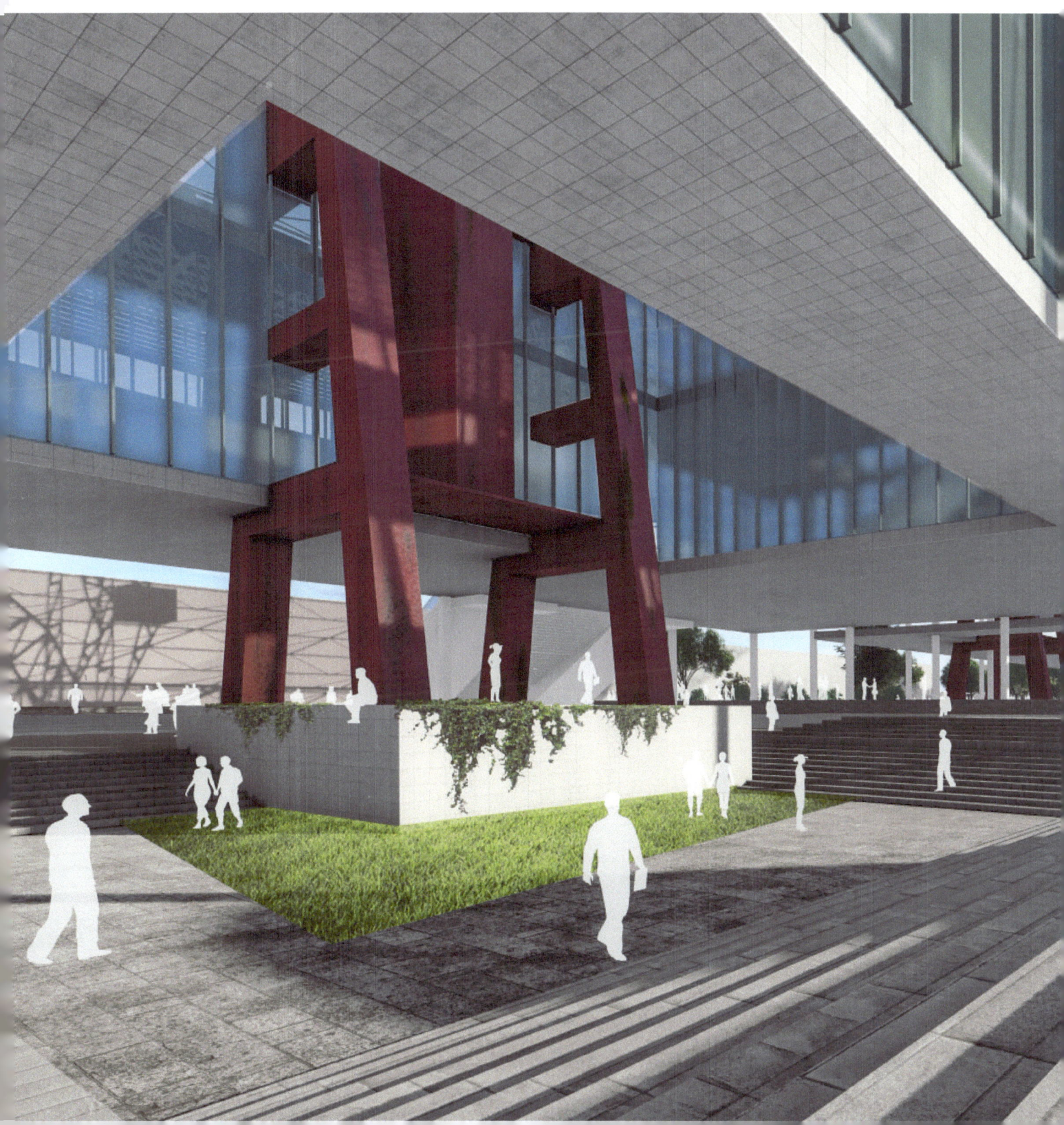

URBAN PARK

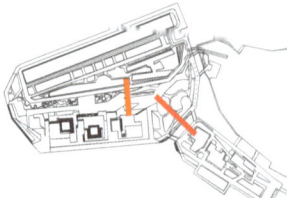

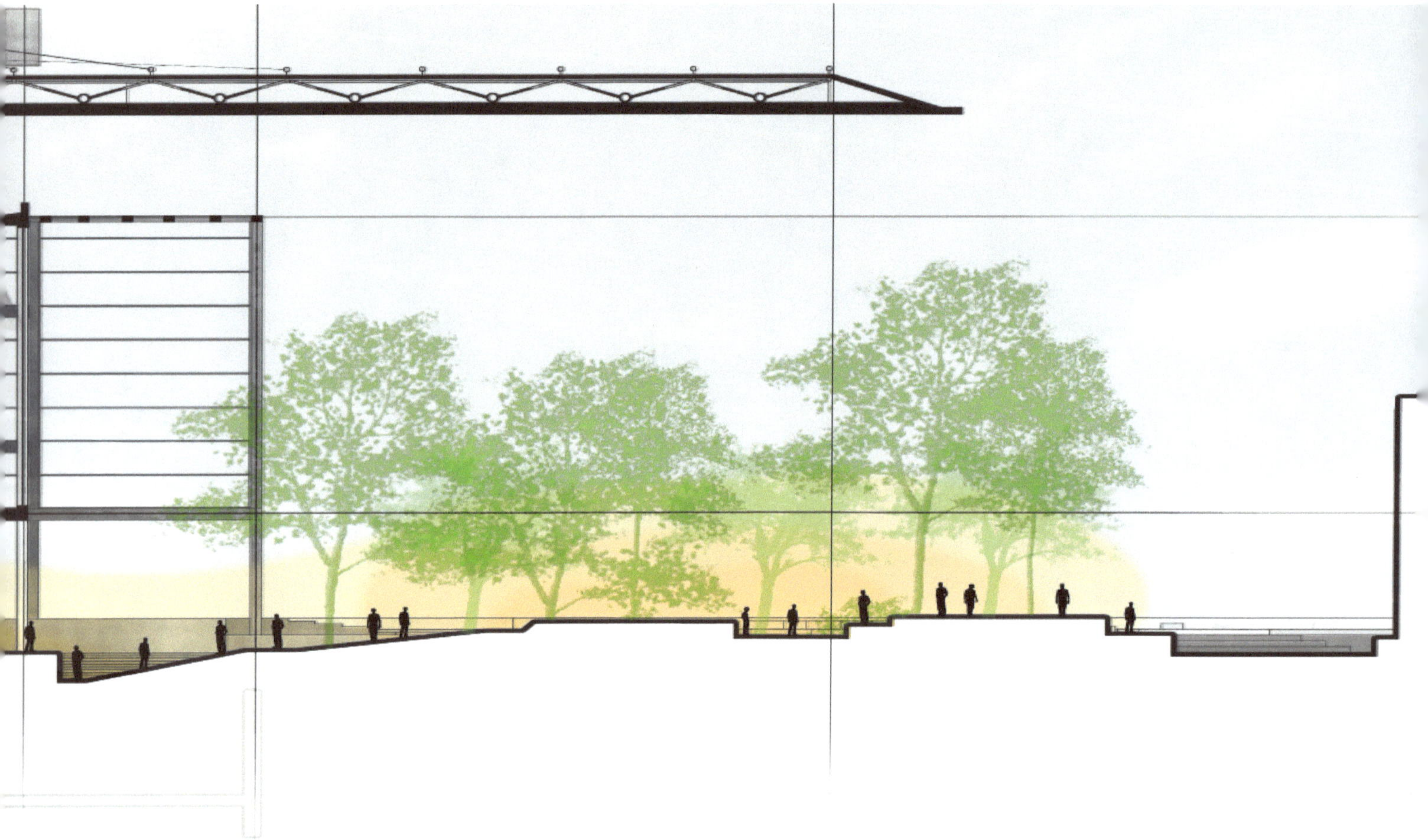

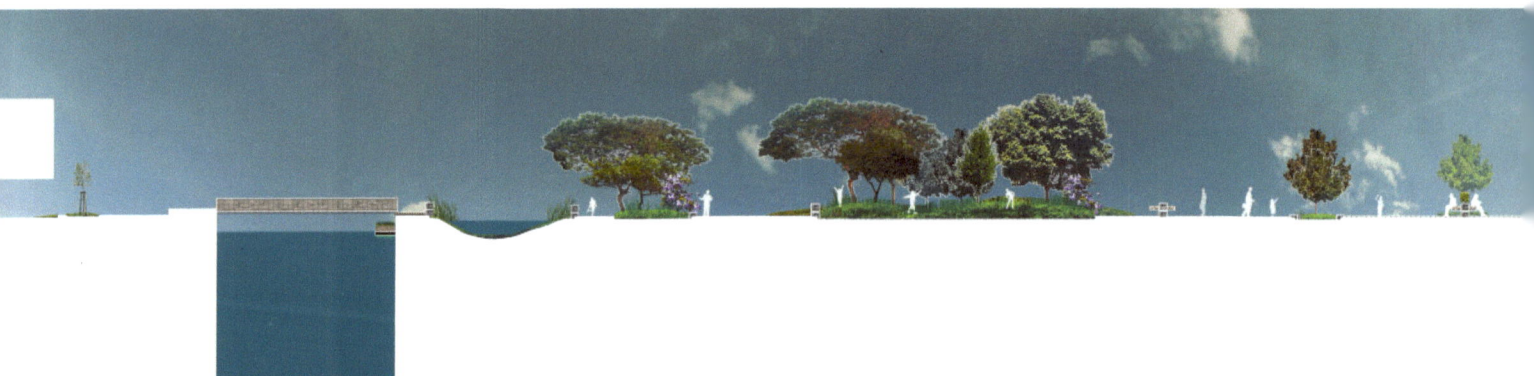

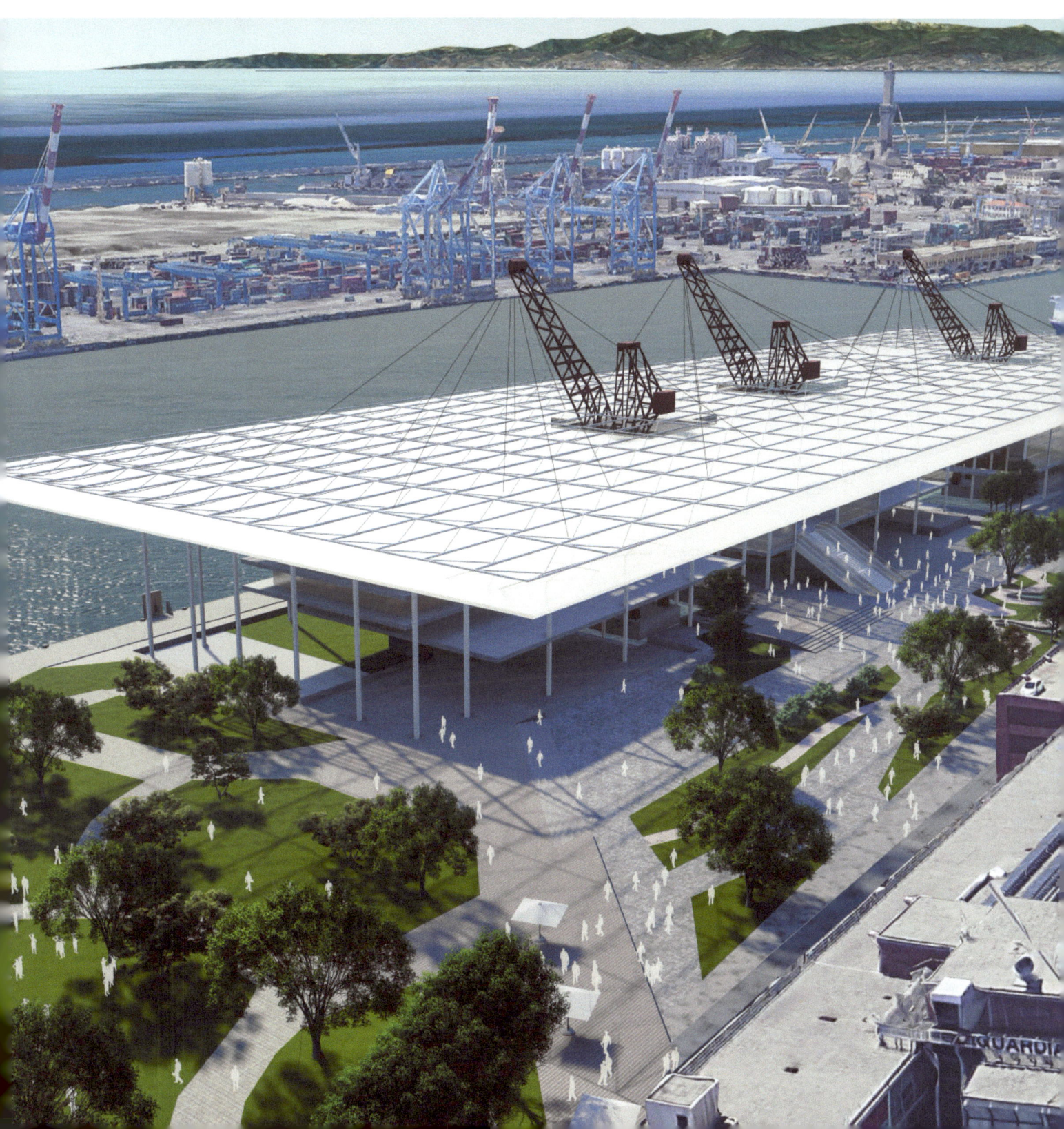

MAIN PUBLIC SPACE
WATERS EDGE

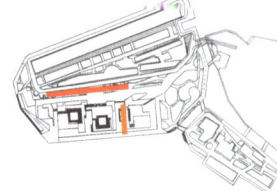

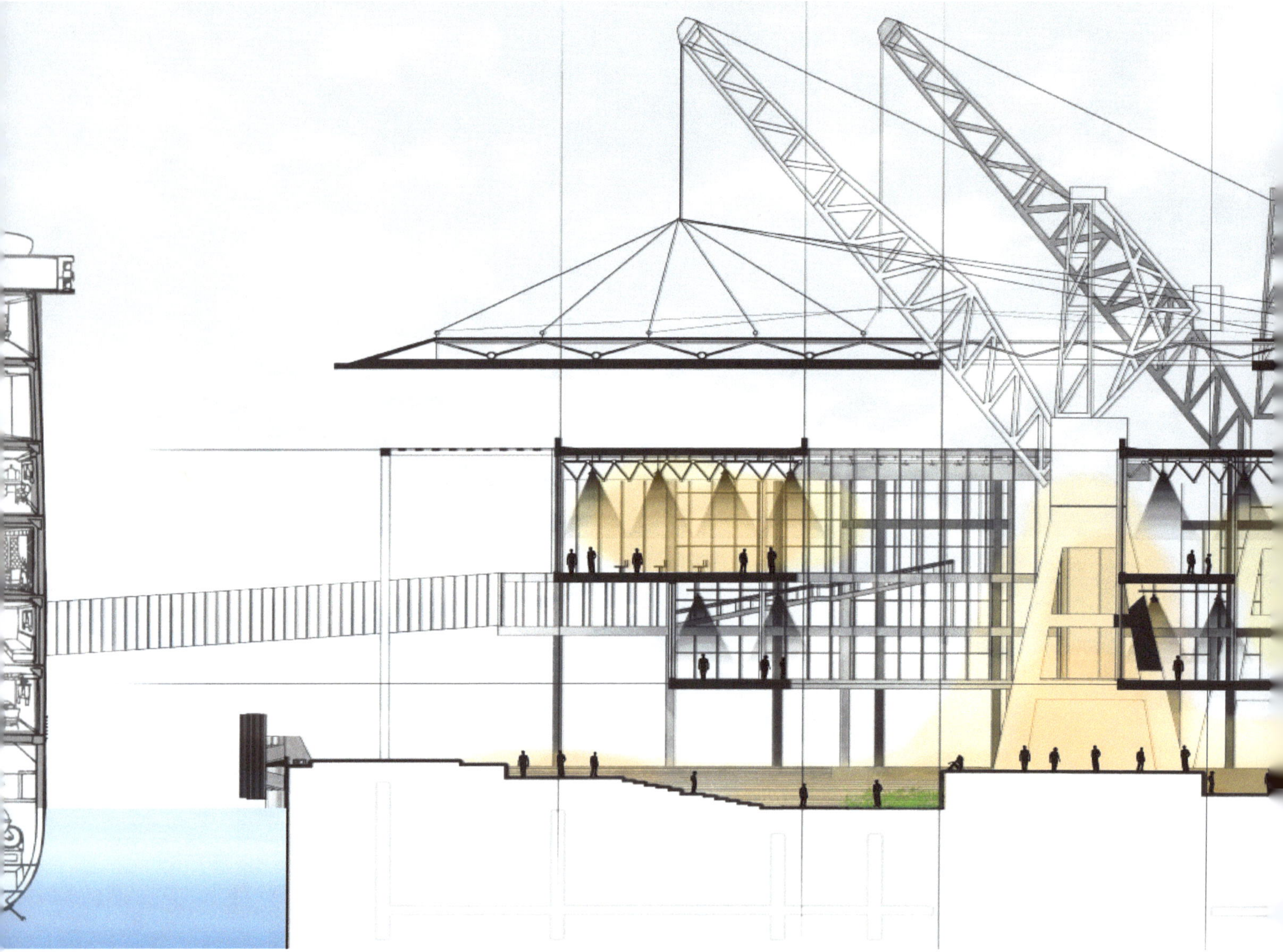

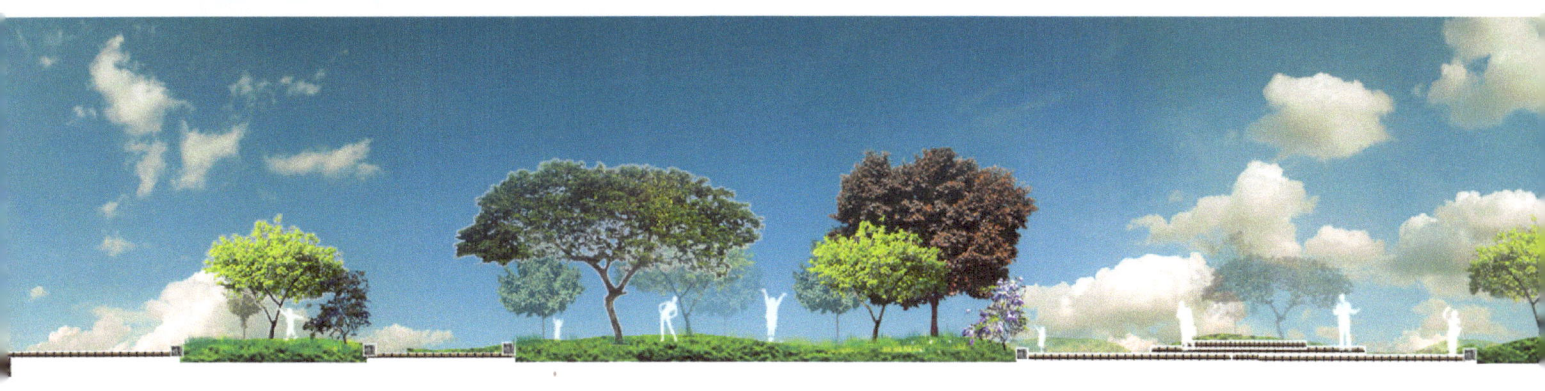

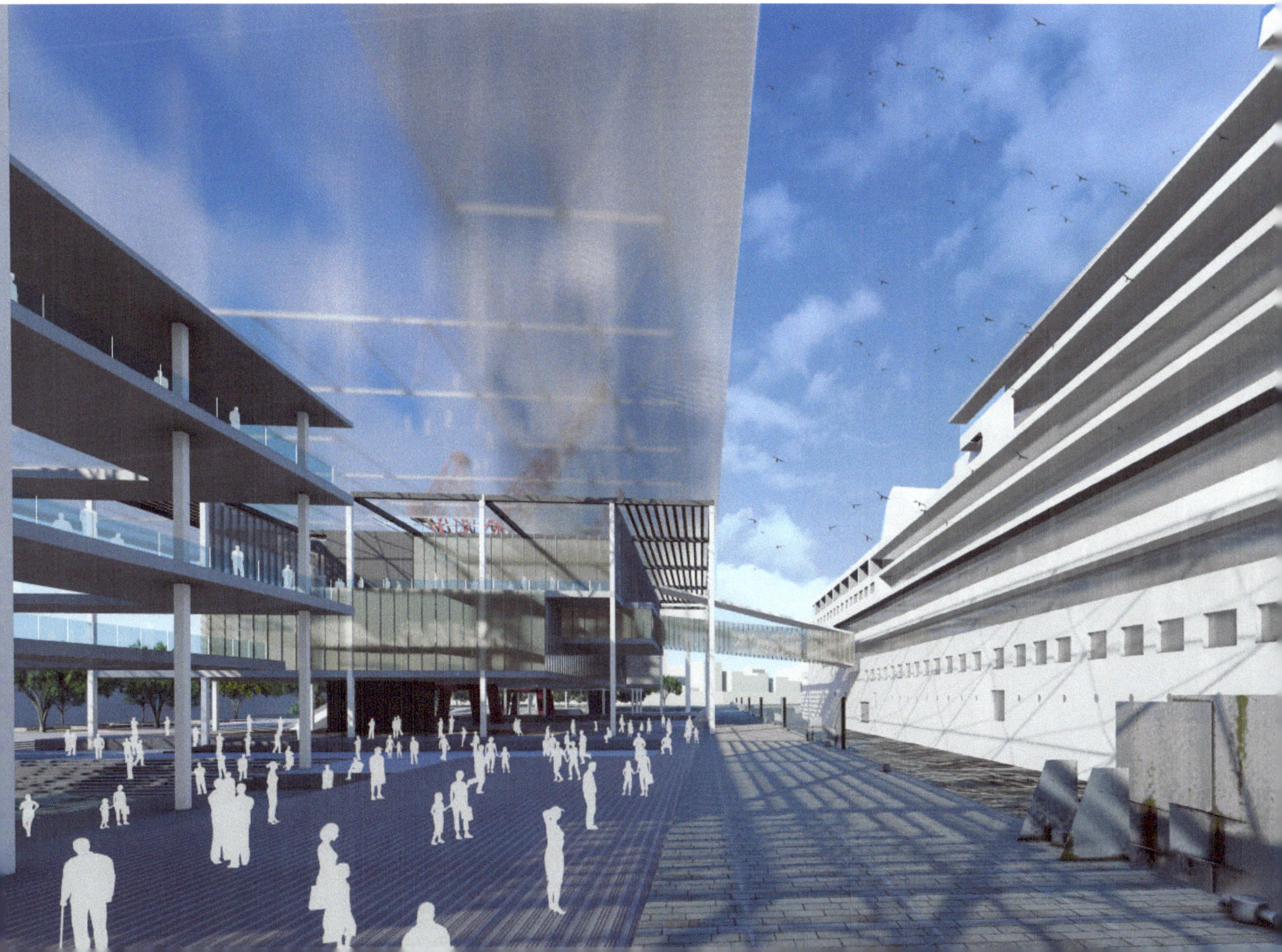

INTERIOR SPACE

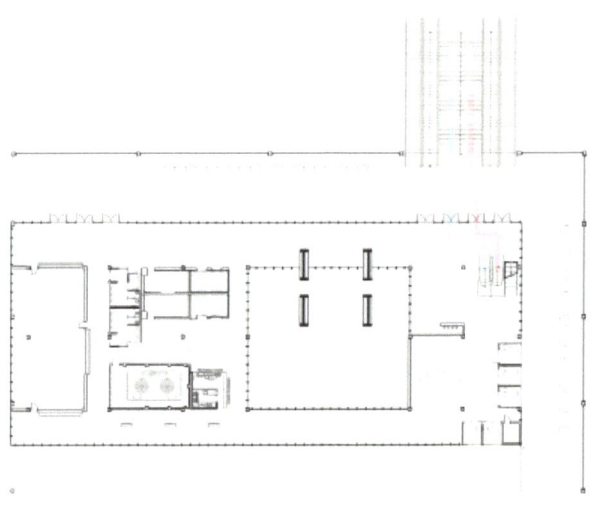

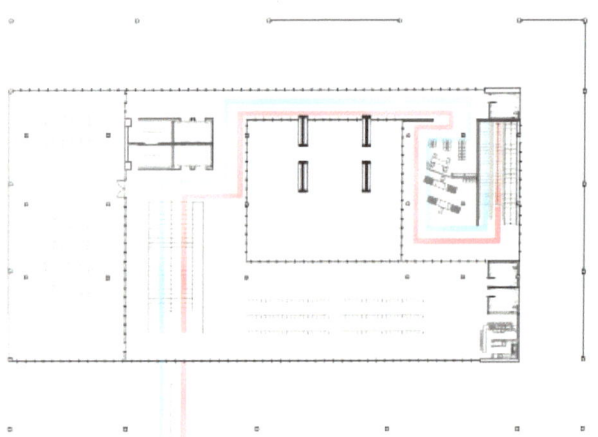

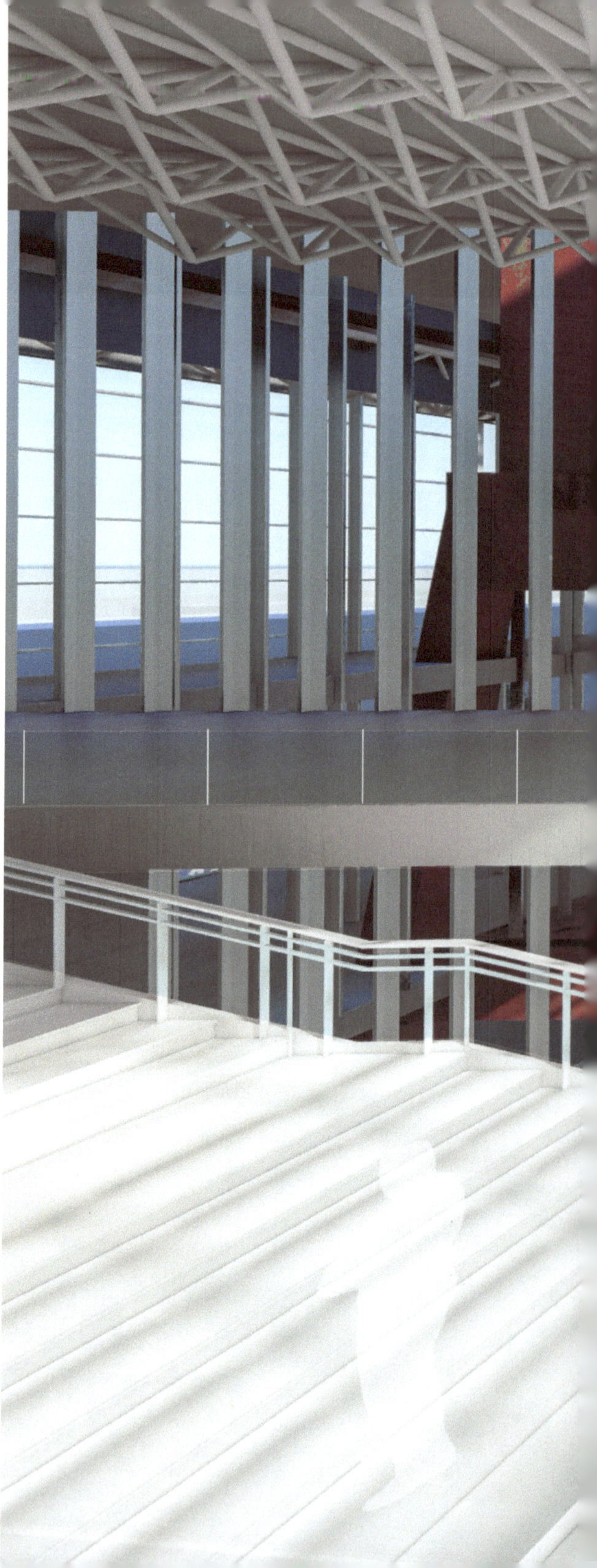

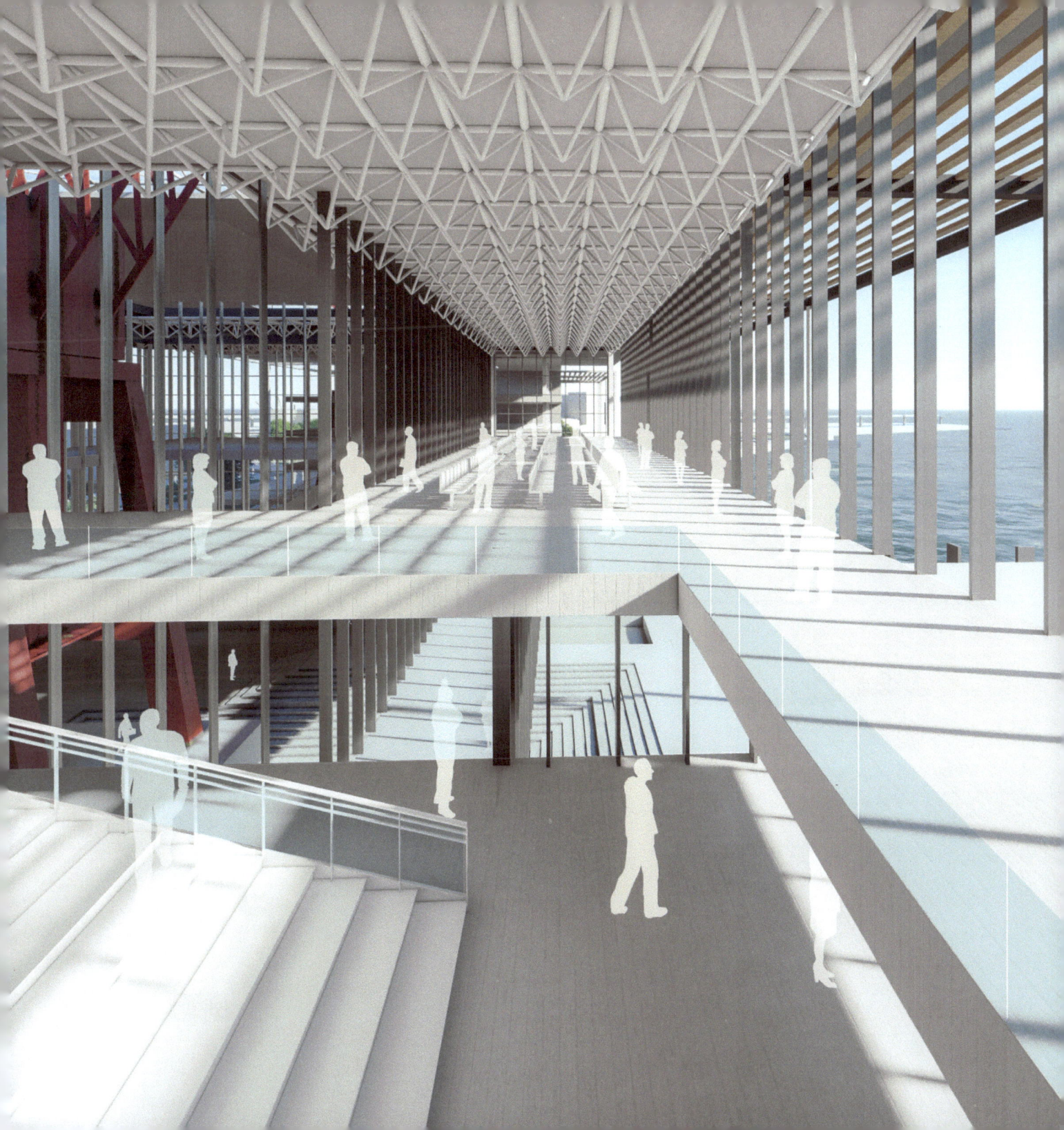

DETENTION POND
Public Atrium during rain events

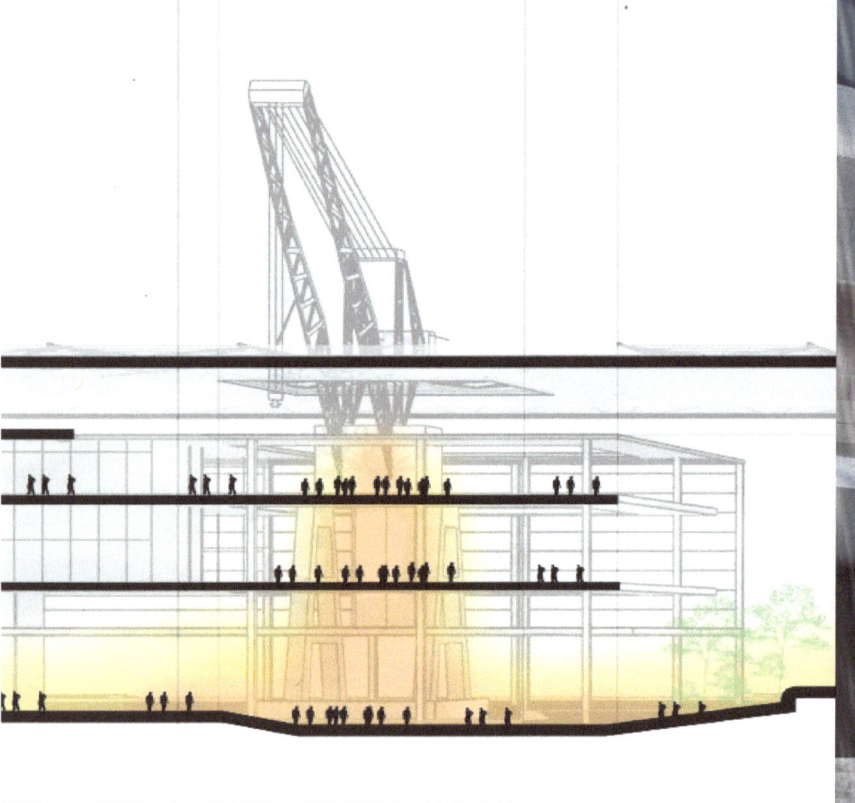

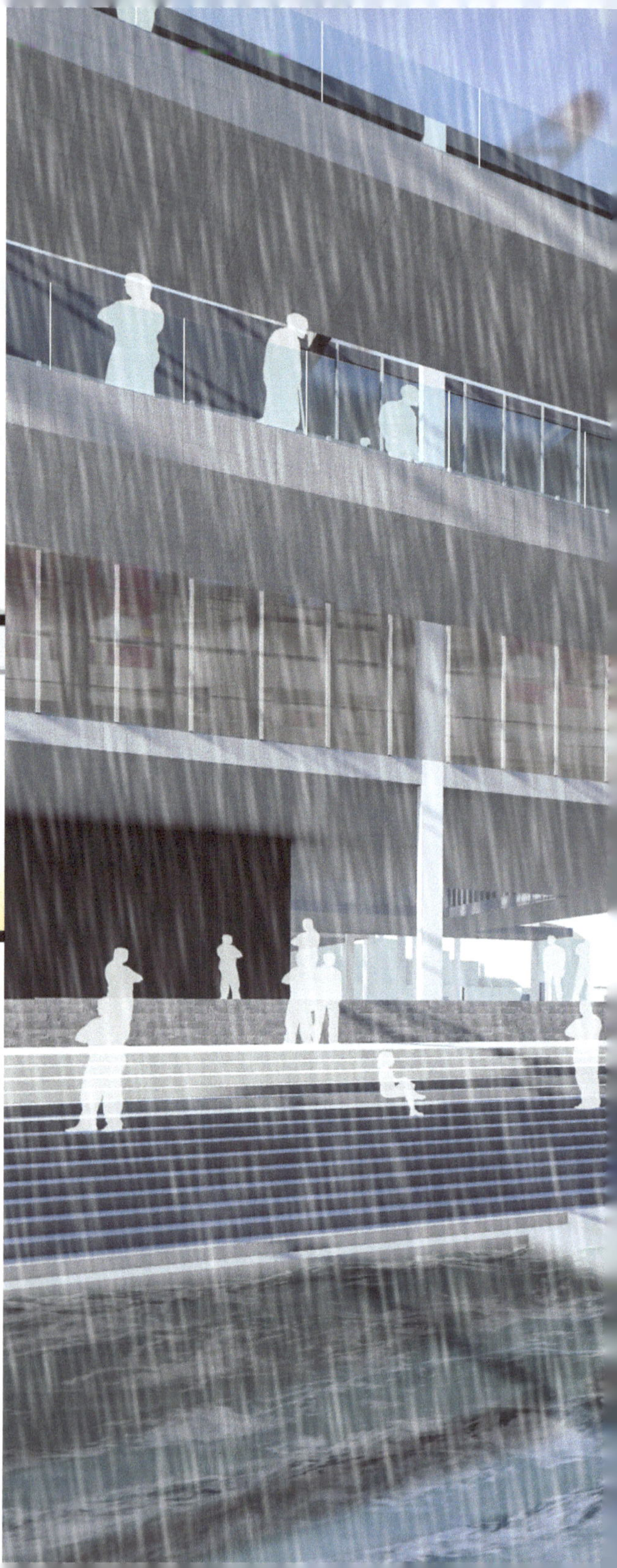

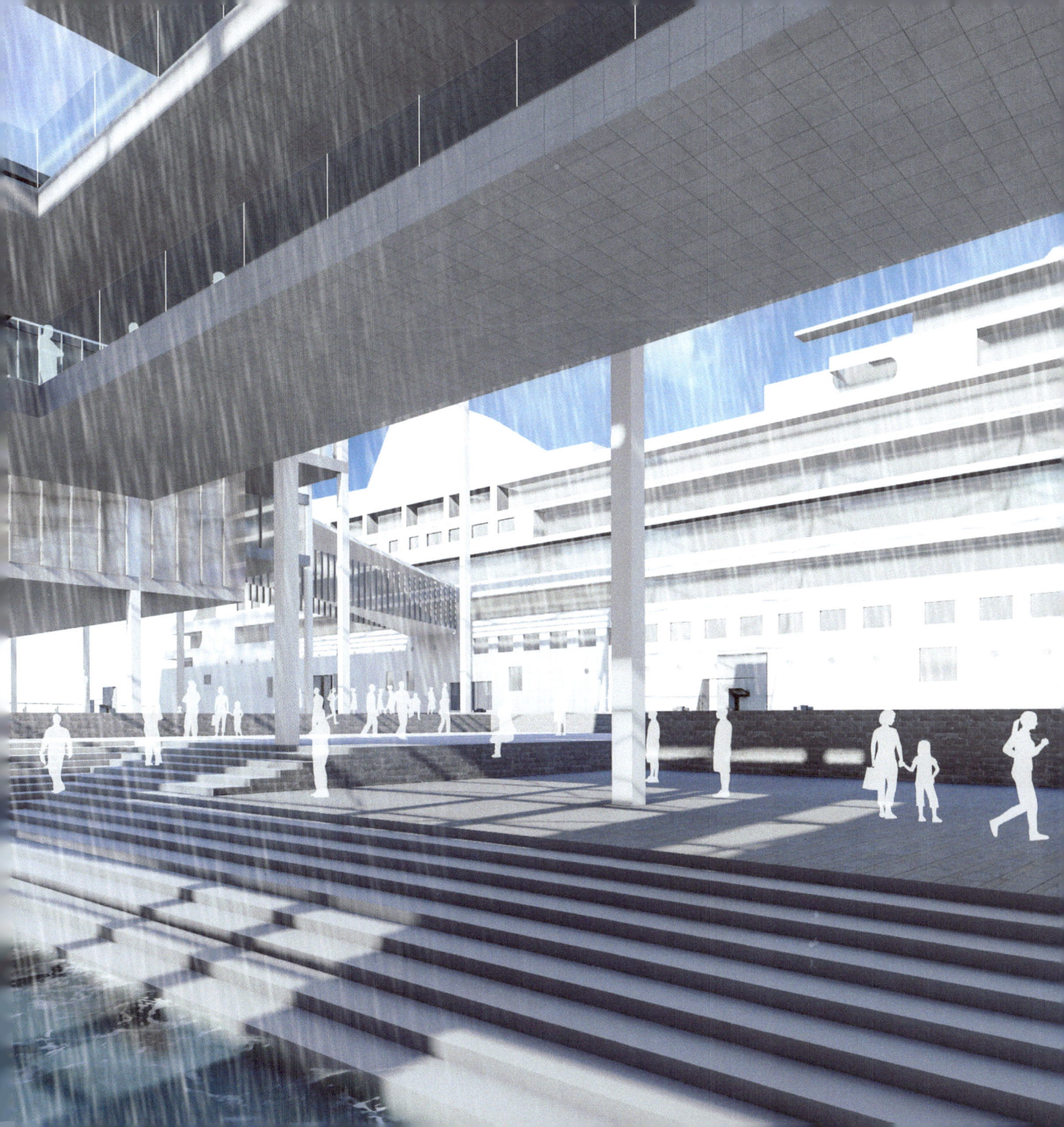

comments

Comments

Comments

Comments

Comments

Comments

Comments